A FANTASY AGO

MOLLY DRINNAN

A
FANTASY
AGO

NEW ZEALAND MEMOIR 1954-56

Matador
9 Priory Busines Park
Wistow Road
Kibworth Beauchamp
Leicester LE8 0RX, UK
Tel: 0116 279 2299
Email: books@troubador.co.uk
Web: www.troubador.co.uk/matador

ISBN 978 1780880 921

British Library Cataloguing in Publication Data.
A catalogue record for this book is available from the British Library.

Typeset by Troubador Publishing Ltd, Leicester, UK
Printed and bound in the UK by TJ International, Padstow, Cornwall

Matador is an imprint of Troubador Publishing Ltd

For Jenny and Shirley and in memory of
Grace and Terry (deceased).

Some of the other names have been changed.

Acknowledgements

My thanks to the Alexander Turnbull Library in Wellington, New Zealand, for sending me information and maps to prod my memory regarding place names, etc.

November 1953

"Hey Grace, what about this," I say, "*free* passage to New Zealand."

It's lunchtime in the offices of the BBC's Audience Research Department at 55 Portland Place, London W.1. Although it is now three months since we returned from the Austrian Tyrol, we're still feeling restless and unable to countenance the thought of once again saving up 15s.0d a week for nine months just to spend a fortnight abroad. Hence our current preoccupation with scanning newspaper advertisements for jobs overseas.

Perhaps, I think, as we mull over the New Zealand idea, I'm destined to go to the Antipodes. Fired with enthusiasm by reading Jean Plaidy's *Beyond the Blue Mountains* when I was 14, I got as far as putting one week's pocket money (2s.6d) in a jar which I labelled 'Australia'.

New Zealand would certainly provide the stepping stone we need and there'd be nothing to stop us from going onto Australia and then perhaps to Canada and America before heading back to Europe and England. We look at each other excitedly: the opportunities for a lifetime of fun and adventure suddenly seem endless and we write off for further details.

The contents of the envelope from the Migration

Branch of the N.Z. Government Offices in Pall Mall are sobering. The enclosed form headed up *Imm.41* tells us that:

> Successful applicants are required to enter into an agreement with the New Zealand Government to remain for a continuous period of two years in the employment to which they are allocated. If an applicant fails to comply with the conditions, he will be required to repay to the New Zealand Government the full amount of the steamship fare(s) paid on his behalf... The purpose of the immigration scheme is permanent settlement in New Zealand.

Two years! That's a long time, but I'm only 18, Grace 22. Then again, we don't like the "...employment to which they are allocated" bit. Although we have lowly jobs at the BBC, we love the excitement of working here and grimace at the thought of being stuck in some boring government department for that length of time. What's more, minimum requirements for shorthand/typists are 100 wpm and 50 wpm respectively. This means the daunting prospect of sitting exams. Naturally, we have to attend an interview, have a full medical and produce employment references. Also, because I'm under 21, I need Mum and Dad's written consent. But am I going to let any of this daunt my resolve to break away from stiflingly suburban Potters Bar and see the world? No. This is a chance of a lifetime and Grace agrees.

At 8 Elmscroft Gardens battle begins. I plead. I weep. I slam doors.

"All right then", I challenge, "if you won't let me go to

New Zealand, perhaps you'll let me get a bedsitter in London like Grace's friend, Oonagh. London's not 12,000 miles away."

This particular idea has been mooted before and rejected on the grounds that I'm too young. Dad tries to reason with me:

"Look at it this way dear – you've got a nice home, a good job and security. Why do you want to throw all that away?"

Now the very mention of the word *security* is enough to banish any doubts or fears that I may have. Surely, I've been asking myself for years, there has to be more to life than hanging wet sheets in the kitchen on a rainy Monday, of turning the bedrooms inside out on Wednesday, of mowing the lawn and roasting beef on Sunday? I absolutely refuse to countenance this way of life.

I fail to understand why Mum and Dad, who are born and bred Londoners, could not wait to escape to the suburbs when they got married, saving up for years and years to get a mortgage. What's more, I find their attitude to their inveterate bookworm, would-be-writer daughter puzzling. They've always been so proud that I was different from the rest of the family – passing the scholarship at 11 (Dad cried with joy), going to Southgate County Grammar School and attaining five 'O' levels.

When I left school in 1951, Dad even wrote to all the national newspapers on my behalf, enquiring whether they had any vacancies for a trainee journalist. The response being negative, he said I would have to settle for a shorthand-typing job in a bank or insurance company. How relieved I was when the local employment agency came up with this job at the BBC. Mum and Dad were thrilled too, but now, two and a half years later, all they see ahead for me are wedding bells, Mum insisting that I'll *know* when the right man comes along. What she doesn't understand is that my Mr Right won't be into wallpapering and growing vegetables: he will be urbane and literary and a world traveller.

Eventually, after Dad has read every word of the immigration papers over and over again, a sort of truce is declared.

"Mum and I have been talking things over," he says, "and if it's really what you want, we won't stand in your way."

December 1953

My inquisitor in the New Zealand Government offices at the Carlton Hotel, Pall Mall is 40 at least and a typical maiden lady, neat and precise in a grey suit and blouse with Peter Pan collar. I sit opposite her on the edge of the chair, hands scrunched together under the table, waiting for her to speak.

"I see you're an only child."

Oh no, not that again. I used to get so sick of the other kids at school assuming that I was spoilt because I had no brothers or sisters.

She looks at me intently.

"You do realise Miss Baxter, that you may never see your family again?"

It's as if she's already guessed that I have no intention of settling permanently in New Zealand.

"Yes, of course."

I'm not good at telling lies and inwardly squirm. Oh what I wouldn't give for the confidence and sophistication of my immediate boss at the BBC, Anne Crone, who sweeps into the office wearing long jangling earrings and a scarf flying from her neck. She was a WAAF during the war, spent two years in Australia after that and now lives in a flat in Kensington.

"And how do you think you'll cope with all the drinking and smoking that goes on in New Zealand?"

Is she trying to frighten me? I declare emphatically that it won't bother me, but just as I'm about to exit the room, she throws a time bomb:

"You know Miss Baxter……"

I turn to look at her.

"….. if I were your parents, I wouldn't let you go."

I drown in despair as I leave the building. Trafalgar Square shimmers through my tears. That's it, isn't it? She's going to reject my application, a suspicion which is reinforced back in the office when Grace, who had her interview a couple of days ago, tells me that nothing was said to her about cigarettes and alcohol and not seeing her family again.

But here I am a few days later jigging for joy when papers arrive for a medical and notification that we have to sit a typing test at the Porten Secretarial College in High Street Kensington. I also arrange to take a shorthand exam at the London Chamber of Commerce.

Friday December 25 1953

Hopefully, this will be my last Christmas day in England for a while. We go to Southgate to spend it with Uncle Bill and Auntie Hilda. I hold them in great esteem because they're the only adults I know who travelled abroad before the war – a two-week cycling tour of Germany in the summer of 1939. Bill is my mother's youngest brother, who was teased unmercifully as a boy by the elder siblings. Mum tells stories of how she and her sister (my Auntie Nell) once shut him in the coal hole and of freewheeling his pram downhill. Today he owns two furniture shops, called *Pounds*, one in Potters Bar and one in Ponders End. As we sit down to dinner I wonder what I'll be doing this time next year.

February 1954

Our medical examinations pass off without any problems, but when we go along after work for the typing tests, I am so nervous I can hardly put my fingers on the keys. Grace, too, is jittery. Nonetheless, we both walk out of the building with a certificate.

March 1954

My shorthand certificate for 100 wpm has come and now – hallelujah – Grace and I receive our hoped-for letters:

Dear Madam,

NEW ZEALAND IMMIGRATION SCHEME
I am pleased to be able to tell you that your application for free passage to New Zealand has

been accepted… Arrangements will be made for you to sail during April/May 1954…

As delighted as we are, we're alarmed at such short notice. This doesn't give us enough time to buy clothes and save up the £20 they advise we take with us – £10 to spend on the voyage and £10 to meet expenses during the time between arrival and our first pay day. We decide to ask if we can go a bit later and as a consequence we are offered a July/August sailing, actual date to follow later. We break the news to our immediate colleagues in Audience Research. They're thrilled for us.

"Oooh," says Doris, "you *are* brave. I couldn't do anything like that."

Later, waiting for the train home at King's Cross, I can't resist telling some of the Potters Bar girls. They're the ones who teased me in my first year at primary school, pulling off my hat and throwing it, one to the other. I was terrified and Mum had to come and meet me for a while. I came into contact with them again three or four years ago at the village hall and youth club dances, but they continue to make me feel socially inadequate because they're pretty and have naturally curly hair which doesn't unravel when it's damp and foggy. They can jive and foxtrot really well, too, so never end up like me, sitting on the sidelines, grinning inanely and trying hard not to mind being a wallflower. I know they think I'm posh because I went to grammar school and work at the BBC and read biographies and things on the train. Now they look at me as if I'm completely mad.

"What on earth do you want to go there for?" says Brenda.

Would I really have expected any other reaction?

April 1954

Something extraordinary happens. For months Doris has been regaling us with stories of this very fashion-conscious girl, Sheila, with whom she regularly travels on the train into London. Well, the other day Doris mentioned to her that two of her work colleagues were off to New Zealand in July – and so it turns out is Sheila. Doris suggests we all meet for lunch in one of the BBC canteens just before we leave.

As if that is not coincidence enough, the whole office erupts with shrieks and yells of delight when a sparkly-eyed Anne Crone sweeps in days later and announces that she, too, is going to New Zealand, but to get married and that she'll be there before us. Anne met Noel when he was over here in the war serving in the air force. She saw him again during her two years in Australia and they have corresponded ever since. Although we won't be able to go to the wedding, we're invited to visit them. This is better than any film scenario and so romantic. All day we return again and again to the subject.

"I just can't believe that the three of you are leaving at the same time and all going to New Zealand," Miss Sendall keeps saying. "My goodness, what are we going to do without you?"

She and Miss Goodall are such nice ladies who lost their fiancés during the 1914-18 war. They're not in the office much because they travel all over the country, training prospective interviewers to go out into the streets to talk to people and ascertain their listening habits. Last year Miss Sendall asked me if I'd like to go out into Portland Place with her and conduct such an interview. I was so thrilled and felt very important clutching my clipboard. She said I did very well.

May 1954

Papers arrive in the post with departure date – July 13 – and lots of other information. Exciting, yes, but I cringe at the thought of telling everyone that we're travelling on the – T.S.S. *"Captain Cook"*: this conjures up a vision of an 18th century convict-carrier.

Another blow – we sail from Glasgow and friends and family will not be allowed on the wharf to wave us goodbye, thus shattering my dream of a band playing and streamers flying as we cast off. Also we have to relinquish our passports which we were so proud to have stamped when we went to Austria; instead we are issued with Documents of Identity.

The really exciting bit – and this makes up for everything – is that the ship "will proceed to New Zealand on the direct route via Curaçao in the Dutch West Indies and the Panama Canal." Caribbean dawns and Pacific sunsets crowd my mental landscape. I go to sleep imagining myself leaning over the deck rail, gazing down into the waters below, the wind blowing through my hair.

Exasperatingly, Dad brings me to earth. All he can do is scrutinise the insurance and baggage forms, the *Notes to Passengers*, et cetera, et cetera. He's such a worrier. I know he'll spend the next few weeks fretting about such things as whether I've got a fraction over the 20 cubic feet of personal luggage allowed and whether the necessary documentation is in order.

Grace and I spend nearly every lunch hour charging up

to Oxford Street in search of clothes. I've now bought a slim-skirted grey suit in C&A for six guineas and high-heeled tan shoes with bag and gloves to match. I'm thrilled to bits with this outfit: surely it will herald the emergence of a more confident and attractive me.

Our last day at the BBC will be Friday 25 June. Anne is also leaving that day and a joint farewell party is being planned for us. At home Mum has decided to have all the family over – or rather those members who talk to each other these days – on Sunday the 27th. Janet and Elaine, the only friends I now have in Potters Bar, will be coming too and, of course, from St. Albans – Dad's favourites – Grace and her two sisters, Mary and Cathy.

It's amazing how their company transforms him. Grace thinks he's super because he makes her laugh and I don't think she believes me when I tell her how unsociable he can be. The number of times I have squirmed in agony when relatives have visited on a Sunday and he has sat silent in his armchair, unable to hide his boredom. Even more embarrassing have been the occasions when someone has struck up a conversation with us on a train or at our holiday guesthouse, Dad immediately frowning and nudging Mum, his warning to her not to get involved. Mum says it's all to do with his childhood, not being wanted and his father going off with another woman and his mother dying young. Also, after having passed a scholarship to attend Regent Street Polytechnic, he had to suffer the humiliation of being forced to leave after a year because the family couldn't afford to keep him there any longer.

Wednesday 2 June 1954

Today Grace and I go along with Doris to the BBC canteen to meet Sheila. She's very pretty and dainty with a tiny waist, accentuated by a wide elastic belt and – wouldn't you know it – naturally curly hair. I bet she'll have all the lads on the ship after her. We get on well, but I have my reservations about us inevitably becoming a threesome. My experience of this in the past has been that it always ends up in a two-against-one situation.

Saturday 5 June 1954

I count the days off, living in a state of feverish excitement punctuated sometimes with middle-of-the-night "Oh, my God, what am I doing?" fears. On this bright, sunny Saturday morning though, I brim with joie de vivre as Dad and I set off for King's Cross to buy a cabin trunk. We have to carry it home between us and as we turn into Elmscroft Gardens, I feel very important and wonder who's watching from behind the net curtains.

Saturday 12 June 1954

I have been off work all week following an adverse reaction to the smallpox vaccination (necessary, we were told, if we wanted to go ashore at Panama). It's been like having a very bad dose of 'flu, with the added discomfort of a swollen and painful arm. I feel nearly my old self today and shall return to work on Monday.

Monday 21 June 1954

A heart-stopping moment at lunchtime: Grace and I are just about to turn into Regent Street on our way back from Oxford Street when I realise I've left my handbag containing all my N.Z. documentation on the counter of D.H. Evans department store. We hurtle back through the crowd. Unbelievably, the bag is where I left it. What would I have done if that had been taken?

BBC Audience Research Department's farewell to (front row, from l. to r.) Grace, Anne, Molly – outside 55 Portland Place, London W1 – Friday 25 June 1954.

Friday 25 June, 1954

Our last day at the BBC and Audience Research does us proud with a splendid party – lots of sandwiches, cakes and sherry. Miss Priestman makes a touching farewell speech.

She's frightfully upper class, just like Daphne and so many of the others, but very friendly and kind. Of course, there have been moments when I've felt uncomfortable about my humble roots, as for example in February 1952 when Daphne and I decided to go to the Mall and watch King George VI's funeral procession. As it would mean a very early start and Daphne lives well into Kent, it was decided she should spend the night in Potters Bar. I was extremely agitated about this. What would she think of my parents? Would Dad behave properly towards her? Would Mum keep asking her if everything was all right? In the event, all went well. They both liked Daphne very much and she in turn liked them. It was the funeral that embarrassed me because just as the hearse was passing us in the Mall I came over faint and had to be treated by the St. John's Ambulance people.

After the speeches Miss Priestman hands out the presents. Grace and I are each given a large flat box, tied with ribbon. Everyone crowds round as we shake out long, floaty, waffle cotton housecoats, blue for me, pink for Grace. They're so pretty and feminine with little bows on the cuffs and a large waist-sash. We try them on and waltz round the office. Anne is given boring old silver teaspoons. Another big moment is when Mr. Silvey, head of the department, calls us into his holy of holies to shake our hands and wish us well.

Finally, we troop down to the ground floor to have photos taken outside. What a tremendous sense of occasion and pride I feel as we stand grouped together on the pavement, dwarfed by the magnificence of this wide, sweeping street – the Royal Institute of British Architects opposite and all the other grand buildings stretching down to Broadcasting House and the Langham.

Inevitably elation is tinged with sadness. I may have been restless and dissatisfied since last autumn, but for the last three years the BBC has been as much a recreation ground for me as a place of work: ice-skating with Grace after work at the Queen's Club in Bayswater; as a member of the 2nd Netball Team, travelling all over the place on Saturday mornings for matches against other companies, then in the summer going down to Motspur Park to play tennis and table tennis. Motspur, too, is where the annual BBC garden party is held. Mum and Dad came last year and were thrilled to witness a performance by the celebrated pianist, Winifred Atwell.

Then, there have been all the free tickets to BBC concerts and radio shows, Mum and Dad again particularly enjoying the occasional Sunday evening in Broadcasting House, listening to the Palm Court Orchestra. And, although music is not my forte, I was especially thrilled to go to a Promenade Concert in the Royal Albert Hall last year.

The farewells are not final for it seems as if the whole office is coming to Euston to wave us off on the night train to Glasgow on July 12. What's more, Misses Sendall and Goodall are going to be in Scotland on business at that time and will try to meet us off the train. They then plan to go and stand on the shoreline and wave to us as the *Captain Cook* sails down the Clyde. This in some way will make up for the disappointment of not having a grand farewell on the quayside.

*Farewell party at home in Potters Bar, Sunday 27 June 1954 –
seated: Mum and Dad; behind from l. to r. Kathy (Grace's sister),
Auntie Ede, Grace, Uncle Bill, Me, Mary (Grace's other sister),
Elaine, Auntie Ett, Janet.*

Sunday 27 June, 1954

I don't remember 8 Elmscroft ever being as full of people as
this and they all come bearing gifts. On Mum's side of the
family there's Uncle Bill and Auntie Hilda and the two
elderly and unmarried dressmaker sisters, Edith and Ethel.
They are always called Ede and Ett – which makes me
cringe.

My favourite aunt is Dad's sister Doris, who was born
with polio and wears an iron caliper on her leg; she is always
so bright and cheerful and interested in what I'm doing. She
arrives with Kitty, the friend she made at work many years
ago and with whom she now lives in Shepherd's Bush. I
greatly admire both of them because they go out a lot to
theatres and films and visit interesting places. I loved

spending the occasional weekend with them in my mid-teens. The only thing I didn't like and which scared me was lying awake in their flat at night listening to the sounds of drunken revelry from the pub down the road.

It's a warm, sunny day so we sit out on the lawn and have lots of pictures taken. Mum puts on her usual teatime spread – ham and tomatoes, celery in a tall fancy glass, tinned peaches and carnation milk, jam tarts, cakes. We go through the usual pantomime, Mum looking worried as she takes up the knife to cut the fruit cake she's made and muttering on about how she hopes it's all right. As always, Auntie Ede says: "oh, it's lovely Doll." But then she and Auntie Ett even go into raptures over bread and butter.

Everybody drifts home about 9 o'clock. It has gone well, Dad has been very sociable and I am content.

Monday 12 July, 1954

I cannot believe that the big day has arrived at last. I felt so strange last week when a large van arrived to take away my trunk duly labelled – **NOT WANTED ON VOYAGE.** It was as if part of me had gone with it. I also have a large suitcase labelled – **BAGGAGE ROOM,** which can be accessed during the voyage and another case for the cabin, containing immediate clothes and toiletries.

In these final moments before leaving the house with Mum and Dad on the first leg of my long journey, I stare solemnly at my reflection in the wardrobe mirror. This part of my life is over and the Molly staring back at me will never be the same again. What will happen to me in the next two years? Shall I still be a virgin? As much as I enjoy heavy petting, I wouldn't dare go all the way before marriage. Apart from the guilt I would suffer at betraying Mum and Dad's trust in me, I'd be absolutely terrified of getting pregnant.

I feel extremely proud and important as Dad shuts the front door and we set off for the station. Surely today neighbours will be watching? Of course, we leave home far too early and have to sit for ages on the platform waiting for the train.

At King's Cross we get a taxi to Euston. This is only the second time I've travelled in one. The first occasion was two years ago when the BBC was holding its 25th anniversary celebrations at Earl's Court Stadium. Four of us, including Grace, had booked in at the YWCA, Tottenham Court Road, because it would be too late to get home afterwards. When we'd bathed and dressed we decided to get a taxi from the hostel to Earl's Court. I remember rushing out into the road with my arm extended, yelling 'taxi, taxi!' just as I'd seen them do in films. It turned out to be an eventful occasion: pea-soup fog halted the entire road transport system and we spent all night in the vast hall, huddled together for warmth because men were laying down ice ready for a skating spectacular to be held the next evening.

We arrive at Euston. How I love the hustle and bustle of railway stations, the smell of smoke, the steam-filled arched roofs, trains shunting in and out, the loudspeaker announcements, whistles being blown and people scurrying hither and thither with cases.

Grace and Sheila and their families soon join us on the platform. Then, true to their word, come all our friends and relations plus a large contingent from the BBC. I swear that we have more people to see us off than anyone else. The hugging and kissing and shaking hands seems endless, but at last the doors are slammed, the whistle blown and the guard hoists his flag. We lean out of the window to wave and the wheels begin to turn. Goodbye London, world here we come.

As we finally flop down into our seats I'm suddenly aware that I'm the only one *not* sniffing and snuffling and furtively wiping her eyes. Good heavens, I'm far too excited to feel sad or to sleep during these long, dark, rushing-to-Glasgow hours. It was the same in 1950 when I did this journey with Mum and Dad. We were going to Dunoon on the Firth of Clyde for our holiday that year. Dad laughed because I had a notebook on my lap all night, recording stations we passed through, then when daylight came, I wrote short descriptions of the scenery. That holiday is blazoned on my memory – such romantic scenery – lochs, waterfalls, hills and then a visit to Edinburgh – the castle and old quarter and Princes Street. I wrote lots of poems about it all and just last week I copied them out into a hard-covered exercise book and presented it to Mum and Dad as a keepsake.

Tuesday 13 July 1954

The moment we hump our cases down onto the platform at Glasgow Central, Grace and I see Misses Goodall and Sendall. They reiterate their intention of finding a spot opposite to where the ship is berthed so they can wave us off. For that purpose each of us has opted to wave a scarf of a different colour. Also, they say, they'll drop a line to our parents to let them know they saw us in Glasgow. We can only chat briefly for we're being directed towards coaches that transport us to a very large first floor restaurant for breakfast.

Soon we're off again for the short ride to the docks and now comes the moment I've been dreaming about for so long – the first sight of the *Captain Cook*. I am not disappointed – such hubbub and activity, decks crowded with sailors, blasts from the funnel, a crane swaying high in the air before being gently lowered into the hold. I can hardly believe that this is *me* – Molly Baxter – waiting in a long queue to board.

Standing behind us is this rather nice-looking fellow, who starts talking to us. His name is Brian and he comes from Kent. Despite Sheila's presence, I'm full of confidence. Is it being away from Potters Bar at last or is it the new hairdo? Grace's sister, Kathy, gave me a super home perm last week – not frizzy but soft and natural. Next thing – this Brian's asking if he can carry my case onto the ship. Dare I hope......?

At the top of the gangplank we give our names to an officer, then we're off, down endless steps, along dark corridors, seeking our cabin. It seems an incredibly small space for Grace and me and, as yet, two unknown companions, but who cares? We choose our bunks, Grace below, me on top. We want to explore the ship before it sails at 11 a.m. so don't bother to unpack.

I'm delighted with everything and very happy at the thought of living like this for nearly five weeks. At the purser's office, we purchase postcards, which will be taken ashore and posted. I scribble one to Mum and Dad:

Here I am bright and breezy sitting in the ship's writing room. It really is so exciting that I don't want you to feel miserable at all. Chin up till you hear from me at Curaçao. Lots of love Molly xxxxx

Afterwards, we go onto the upper deck where there's a huge crush of people. Sheila appears and the three of us follow the example of some young guy who's clambered up on top of a stack of life rafts to get a better view.

The world jostles at our feet, but as I listen to scraps of conversation, I suddenly feel deflated – *not* because I'm leaving Britain, but because up to this moment I've felt so proud of being one of the 'chosen.' Now looking around me I begin to wonder why so many of the men were selected. They're certainly not like those we knew at the BBC; some of them are even reminiscent of the Teddy boy types who live up the rough end of Potters Bar.

I'm soon distracted though, for here's Brian scrambling up to join us. He offers us all a cigarette. I take one. This is the first time in my life I feel free to indulge openly, not that Mum and Dad minded too much, but it seemed to me that some of the older BBC women disapproved.

What with being so excited at the thought of our imminent departure and Brian standing close to me, I can't believe my ears when just below us I hear a woman *complaining* about the size of her cabin. Imagine, having something so mundane on your mind when the funnel's blasting, the ropes are being slipped from the bollards and *Now is the Hour* is sounding out from a gramophone? Dear God, do these people have *no* sense of occasion?

As we turn into the mainstream of the Clyde, Grace and I, scarves ready, strain our eyes towards the opposite shoreline, then it's –

"Grace, look", and grabbing her arm, "surely, that's them."

Whether Misses Sendall and Goodall have managed to spot us, God knows, but we wave for as long as they're in sight.

It's a slow business sailing down this huge, swarming river flanked by vessels from all over the world. Such a clamour comes from them, such a drilling and hammering and ringing of steel. Strung in cradles down the sides there are men slapping paint on bulwarks. Hooters blast in farewell and sailors lean on deck rails to wave to us. Someone shouts out:

"Ye'll be back – ye'll be back."

What's he talking about? *Of course* we'll be back.

We begin to feel chilly. Most people wander off, but we stick it out until the Atlantic looms ahead, then return to the cabin where Helen, as she introduces herself, is neatly stacking underwear in one of the drawers. My spirits sink: she's thirty at least and looks so prim with her blonde hair scraped into a bun. Although Rosemary, our other travelling companion, freckled and quietly spoken, is not exactly our idea of fun either, at least she's our age.

Grace and I get ready for dinner. We're on first sitting for meals, Brian and Sheila on the second. The dining room to which we have been allotted is large and noisy, everyone talking at once, but oh how grand it feels to be part of such a scene and waited on by a steward. Tonight, after second sitting, there's dancing to gramophone records in the lounge. I feel anxious at the prospect. Although there are plenty of blokes aboard, will they be interested in me and what about Brian? I'm not one hundred per cent sure it's me he likes and I can't bear the thought of being a wallflower.

My stomach churns as we make our way to the lounge, especially when I see Sheila looking as pretty as ever and flashing her eyes at Brian. Then, to my dismay, because there's not enough seating for everyone, she plonks herself down on his lap. Well, that's my fate decided. I take another cigarette, even though I don't want it, and set my face into its familiar 'I'm having fun and I'm not jealous' grin. What happens next is unbelievable. Brian suddenly shoos Sheila from his lap and asks *me* to dance. Overwhelmed with happiness and gratitude, I skim away with him over the floor not even wrong-footing as I've done so many times in the past when I've felt nervous and self-conscious. Even better is Brian keeping tight hold of my hand when the bracket of dances finishes. We spend the whole time together and on deck afterwards he tells me how much he likes me.

"I thought it was Sheila you were keen on," I blurt out.

"Didn't I make it obvious it was you? ", he says, surprised.

We start to snog and I'm transported. What a day!

Thursday 15 July 1954

The third day into the voyage, the sky is still grey, the sea wild and the lounges full of people playing cards and writing letters. Grace and I, however, decide to brave the elements. We put on our windcheaters, go right up to the front of the ship where we hold on tight to the rail. All around us the sea's heaving and hollowing and we cannot hear ourselves speak above the wind. A wave slaps over the bow, showering us with spray. It happens again. We're soaked but we don't care. I've never known such exhilaration, such intense joy. I feel as if I'm suspended in space. When I think of Mum and Dad and everyone else stuck at home, I pity them from the bottom of my heart. It's become apparent though that not everyone shares our sense of adventure and delight for we hear constant moans about the size of the cabins, the food and the weather.

"There's nothing to do," people whine.

Yes, it's true, deck space is cramped and there's no swimming pool, but isn't just being aboard a ship bound for the other side of the world via the Dutch West Indies and the Panama Canal enough?

T.S.S. "Captain Cook", Forward Dining Saloon

T.S.S. "Captain Cook", Lounge

Tuesday 20 July 1954

I don't even want to think about being on dry land again for I've never been happier than aboard my ocean-bound home with Brian constantly in tow. He's started to talk about a future together, even though I'll be living in Wellington and he, like Sheila, will be based in Auckland. Despite a feeling of unease because – let's face it – he's not exactly the sort of bloke I envisaged as a husband – I'm immensely flattered and can't help getting carried away by the idea.

Now the weather is brighter we get up on deck as much as possible – Grace and Sheila, John and me. We've become friendly, too, with a jolly couple – Jack and Irene and their two lovely little girls, Maureen and Beverley.

Sheila, Grace and me on deck of T.S.S. "Captain Cook"

Thursday 22 July 1954

Oh dear, reality has at last impinged upon this idyllic existence for the day has come to go down to the communal laundry. I've never done any washing before, Mum preferring to do it all herself on a Monday.

Friday 23 July 1954

Although the washing turned out to be easy, I have a problem with the ironing. Having waited for ages for a board to become vacant, I feel nervous about getting down to the task, especially as Helen is one of several in the queue with eyes fixed on me. As I try unsuccessfully to get the creases out of a blouse, I become more and more self-conscious and decide to come back later. Imagine my surprise, therefore, when I return to the cabin late this afternoon and see my skirts and blouses hanging up and all beautifully ironed.

"Hope you didn't mind," says Helen, who is lying on her bunk reading a book, "only I had nothing to do."

I feel embarrassed, but thank her over and over again.

Tonight Judy, one of the girls we've got to know, invites us and others to her cabin before dinner to drink a bottle of sherry she smuggled aboard. We have great fun, all squashed into every conceivable space, sitting on the bunks, on the floor. This is the sort of boarding school camaraderie that I read about as a child. The sherry has to go a long way, but Judy passes out. My Dad couldn't take drink either. I remember him being sick after some celebration where he'd drunk only two glasses of beer. Mum has a sherry at Christmas, but really she hates booze because her father drank the money he made from his boot and shoe business. She's often told me how she and her sisters would lie petrified in bed, waiting for him to come home from the pub.

Judy recovers, but feeling poorly decides to sleep instead of eat. Grace and I, however, are in high spirits and drift off to the dining room. Afterwards, as usual, I position myself at the top of the stairs of Brian's dining room and wait for him to come up. The stewards tease me unmercifully, but I lap it up.

"Here's the love bird again," they say.

Sunday 25 July 1954

We sight the coast of Venezuela. Curaçao is not far off. A boat skims over the sea and comes alongside the ship. The pilot will guide us into Wilhelmstadt. How can those around me remain so calm and uninterested when I'm fizzing with excitement? Nonetheless, as we move amongst the great tankers and other vessels at anchor, the heat of the day and the sickening smell of oil overpower me and I feel miffed because Brian is not coming ashore with us: he wants to go off and drink with his cabin mates.

As much as I wanted to share this experience with him, I refuse to let my disappointment spoil the thrill of stepping ashore, of walking over the pontoon bridge to get to the shopping area of the town, of seeing big American cars glide past us. Under the blue sky and burning sun everything is bright and light and white. Buildings are wooden and gabled in Dutch style and some of the streets, which are no more than alleys, are bordered with little shops, name signs swinging above them – Sombreros Parizza; Holeproof Hosiery; Casa Cohen. As for the people, I love the children with their jet-black hair and white gleaming teeth and remember the album of coloured postcards Dad brought home from the Bahamas where he was stationed in the war. Impossible it seemed then that I would ever visit such a place.

We only have enough time here to go for a drink in the Seamen's Mission. This is adorned with three gabled peaks, the steps leading up to the entrance flanked by flags and flowering trees. We buy souvenirs – penknives and bangles and postcards to send home. Back on ship we watch the whole fascinating process of lifting anchor and edging slowly towards the open sea. Soon Brian appears by my side and I feel an enormous sense of relief.

Wednesday 28 July 1954

At 10 o'clock this morning we enter the Panama Canal, a hot, sticky world of jungle, of heat-misted lakes and lochs such as that in which the ship is now entrapped. We're all crowded on the deck watching the water rise higher and higher, waiting for the gates ahead to swing back so that we can move onward. When they do, we enter a narrow seaway flanked by a tangle of thick green vegetation – rubbery-looking plants and palm fronds, dark, mysterious and rustling. The air is thick. At odd moments we hear the chatter of monkeys. This is even more exciting than Curaçao and I feel like a pioneer. At 6 p.m. we anchor in Balboa.

On this occasion Brian is coming ashore with me, together with Grace, Sheila and John – our jolly little dining-room waiter. The ride into Panama City in a rickety old contraption they call a bus is a bone-rattling experience.

Bumping up and down, tossed from side to side, we wonder if we'll arrive in one piece.

As in Wilhelmstadt, wooden buildings line the streets and white faces are in the minority. Waiter John, a seasoned Panama visitor, introduces us to thick, steaming hamburgers, then takes us to a bar called The Washington where some fellow passengers are already installed. There's a jukebox against one wall and someone has pressed the button for *Three Coins in the Fountain*. We order rum and coke. What could possibly be more romantic than this? Soon though we're heading back to the ship on the thrill-a-minute bus. My head spins with excitement. On board gossip is rife: one of the crew was involved in a drunken fight ashore.

Friday 30 July 1954

The Pacific Ocean dazzles as we take our places this morning for square dancing on the aft deck. Entranced and exhilarated, I skip, jig, twirl and clap my hands. Life is simply wonderful.

Mid-afternoon I'm leaning over the ship's rail, rapt in watching a broadening trail of white foam spread out behind us when someone shouts:

"Look!"

Out of the dark blue depths leaps a flying fish, then another and another. What bliss to think that there are three more weeks of this and for the nth time I wonder why so many fellow passengers are bored with life aboard ship.

Saturday 31 July, 1954

Today, sitting up on deck, I get to know the dynamic, full-of-fun Jennifer Foley. We hit it off at once. She comes from Bristol, has a lilting West Country accent, and is very attractive – huge brown eyes and brown pageboy-styled hair. Because she doesn't celebrate her 18th birthday until 12 August, she's under the supervision of liaison officers who will also help her to find employment in Wellington.

Jenny and me on deck of T.S.S. "Captain Cook"

Sunday 1 August, 1954

We are about to pass over the equator. Waiter John tells us that on fare-paying ships, crossing the equator is really something. Everyone dresses up and goes through an initiation ceremony. This can involve being pelted with flour, et cetera and thrown into the swimming pool. As I've never enjoyed horseplay, I'm happy enough with our makeshift do – an officer dressing up as King Neptune and handing each of us a certificate, which reads:

Tuesday 3 August, 1954

Brian is cooling off. I can no longer overlook the familiar signs which heralded the demise of my first love, Christopher, when I was 15. Today when I see him flirting with this sexy-looking blonde on deck I can bear it no longer. I escape to the cabin to cry my heart out.

Friday 6 August 1954

I have to keep drumming into my head that when we disembark on 19 August, Brian will be out of my life, but given my passionate, all-or-nothing nature, I find it hard to put on a brave face. Jenny, however, helps me enormously. She's such a get-up-and-go, wide-open person and in her company I get swept up in her zest for life.

We flirt madly with the stewards and waiters and have even become friendly with the ship's doctor who asks if we'd like to assist him with some clerical work. This afternoon I do some typing for him. Zipping down the corridor after leaving his cabin, a hand suddenly reaches out of a side pantry and pulls me into it.

"Got yer!" says the big fat steward we've nicknamed Teddy Bear. "Give us a kiss."

"Help! Help!" I shout in mock indignation, which brings Jenny running back to join in the fun.

Saturday 7 August, 1954

I'm in a panic. It's the Fancy Dress Parade tonight and my sewing skills are negligible.

"Don't worry," Jenny says, "I'll help you."

We spend the afternoon in her cabin with some of the other girls, surrounded by articles of clothing and scarves and crêpe paper which we purchase at the purser's office. Jenny transforms herself into a gypsy while I become a 1920s flapper girl. The trouble is that it's breezy up on deck as we gather for the parade and my flimsy crêpe skirt begins to tear. I clutch at it frantically as we shuffle along the deck, but by the time judging takes place I look a disaster. Some of the costumes are truly original. Dizzy, the madcap woman in Jenny's cabin, looks splendid as a veiled harem dancer. She wins first prize.

Friday 13 August 1954

Drifting along in this world of sea and sky for over four weeks, past and future have had no substance. Never once have I felt homesick or yearned to reach New Zealand and even now, with the Farewell Dinner imminent, I shut my ears to those who are speculating on what lies ahead once we reach land. If only I could spend the rest of my life aboard ship, travelling the world....

Saturday 14 August 1954

The dining room tonight is decorated with garlands and streamers. A souvenir menu lies beside each place setting. On offer is:

Tomato Juice Cocktail

Crème Argenteuil

Fried Fillets of Sole, Lemon

Spaghetti Milanaise

Roast Turkey Savoury Stuffing

Garden Peas, Roast & Boiled Potatoes

Braised York Ham

Corned Ox Tongue

Crisp Lettuce Parmentier French Dressing

Ice Cream & Fruit Salad

Rolls, Tea Coffee

There's a tremendous sense of togetherness. After we've finished eating, we wander from table to table asking people to autograph our menu cards – fellow passengers, waiters and even the ship's commander, Captain Alexander Bankier. I'm tickled pink by some of the messages written on mine – "See you in my dreams" and "To the blonde who isn't dumb".

Monday 16 August 1954

The colder weather reminds us that we're going into the New Zealand winter. The ship changes countenance, a shut down atmosphere beginning to prevail as we pack away our summer clothes. Even I begin to speculate on the future. What will the hostel be like? Grace and I have always envisaged it as a sort of redbrick YWCA on the lines of the one in London's Tottenham Court Road.

Thursday 19 August 1954

Our last breakfast aboard and afterwards we all go up on deck to await our first sight of *The Land of the Long White Cloud* as the Maoris call New Zealand. The sea is grey and choppy this chilly morning and when the first rocky outcrop appears on the horizon, I have a strong sense of having reached the end of the world. Maybe everyone feels like that because there's little chatter as the pilot boat takes us through the Heads.

On the starboard side the shoreline is back-dropped with hilly terrain, at first denuded of vegetation, but then gradually becoming greener and finally interspersed with white weatherboard houses. On the port side the hills are of gentler incline and there are more habitations, but it's what I term a nothing-happening landscape, which is pervaded by a vast calm. Even as we ease at last into the quayside and the city is before us and around us and there are people on the wharf, there's still an inescapable sense of quiet and strangeness.

Once the gangways are put in place officials come aboard to begin the process of checking us off. We say goodbye to those destined for Auckland, including Sheila who hopes to see us again sometime. Happily, I feel unperturbed when Brian takes my hand and wishes me well.

Coaches are on the wharf to transport us to our new home. We start the journey in good spirits, but the banter soon ceases when we realise that we're not driving *into* town but away from it. Where on earth are they taking us?

"Well, it can't be far off now," says a girl at the back.

Her optimism is short-lived and the inveterate grumblers start to protest as we travel on and on through a landscape of green hillsides and white wooden bungalows. At long last the coach veers off onto a side road and swings into a compound consisting of rows of Nissen huts. This is Trentham Immigration Hostel – the end of our 12,000 miles journey.

Near the entrance is the administrator's office, the canteen and lounge. Flanking the complex are the living quarters, one side for men, one for women. Down the middle are facility huts, bicycle sheds, etc. Each hut has two communal bathrooms off a long corridor, either side of which are small, unheated rooms, sparsely furnished with two single beds, wardrobe and dressing table.

Some of the girls are in tears. Many of them, including Grace, declare their intention of getting out and into a flat as soon as possible. This poses a dilemma for me. I enjoyed communal living on the ship and very much want to continue it. If we move into town now, we'll be isolated. Jenny feels the same way. Although I feel guilty about splitting up from Grace, we agree that there's no other solution. I shall therefore share a room with Jenny and Grace will move into town.

Several of us decide to go into Wellington by train this afternoon. This proves an illuminating experience. Apart from the racecourse, Trentham has one café on the road leading to what is called a station. This is nothing more than a narrow platform, reached by walking across the railway lines. Our legs and feet start to itch like mad. The culprits, we learn later, are sand flies. When the train arrives, we scramble aboard onto one of the open tin-plated platforms that separate each of the long carriages. Jenny cannot contain her hilarity:

"My God," she yells, swaggering aboard, with hands on her hips "it's like the Wild West".

This feeling of being cut off from the world persists even when we leave the Hutt Valley and the harbour comes into view. However, although Wellington station is much quieter than London's rail termini, the building is large and impressive with central columns and landscaped forecourt. On the other side of this trams arrive and depart.

Jenny and I venture up Lambton Quay. Here shop roofs, supported by pillars, project over the pavement at first-floor level, providing shelter for pedestrians on wet days. On the left-hand side is a department store – the DIC. We have an inclination to knit jumpers, so we make for the wool counter and debate whether we should we spend some of our remaining £10. But remembering that the authorities have offered an advance to tide us over to our first payday, if necessary, we make purchases.

Friday 20 August 1954

Today we learn where we'll be employed for the next two years. Grace is going to work for the State Hydroelectric Department, Jenny at the Gas Board, while I've been assigned to the New Zealand Government Tourist and Publicity Department on Lambton Quay. That sounds very exciting.

Sunday 22 August 1954

As our first weekend in New Zealand draws to a close and we huddle together around a huge, old-fashioned stove in the lounge, we know that life at Trentham is going to be spartan. The self-service canteen food is ghastly – grey meat swimming in gravy, soggy vegetables, mashed potato, steamed puddings, lumpy custard. We are not allowed heaters, cooking apparatus or the opposite sex in our rooms, although I understand these rules are often ignored. For instance, there are two older women, factory workers, who spend every non-working hour in their rooms, brewing pots of tea. They go round with their hair permanently in curlers and wrapped in headscarves, cigarettes hanging from their lips, gossiping about everyone. Despite all this, I relish the challenge of living here for a while.

Monday 23 August 1954

As we set off from Trentham for our first day at work in Wellington, I feel just as nervous as I did when heading for the BBC in August 1951. But as it was then, everyone is so friendly, although I find the overall boss, Mr Odell, a small, bald-headed man with dark penetrating eyes, intimidating. I'm relieved that his secretarial work is done by my office companion, Hilary, a posh Englishwoman of about 30, who reminds me of Daphne at the BBC. Hilary spent a year working aboard a ship in the purser's office before ending up here. She seems very pleasant and helpful. I'm going to be doing general typing – press releases, travel articles, et cetera for all the journalists working in the Publicity Division and also have to take shorthand from Odell's deputy, Mr Scully. He, too, is scary with fierce bushy eyebrows and ginger-coloured moustache, but Hilary says he's okay.

Friday 27 August 1954

As thrilled as I am with office life, it's nice to have the first working week over. Back at camp we're settling down into a routine and beginning to form friendships. I very much like Shirley Harrison, who's a Londoner and works in an insurance office. Then there's blonde Terry Harbron from

Portsmouth, employed by the Dairy Board; she's good fun but much more sophisticated than the rest of us. Another blonde, Bettie, has such a broad Scots accent I can hardly understand her at times, while Linn, dark and slim and very careful of her appearance, hails from Hornsey in North London where Mum was born.

Tonight in the lounge I have a super game of table tennis with one of the English boys. Then Jenny, who this last week has established herself as life and soul of the party, gets up on the table and performs a tap-dance routine. What I wouldn't give to have her self-confidence and ease in talking to men.

Happy days at Trentham Immigration Hostel – front row: Linn; second row l. to r: Jenny, me, Bettie, third row l. to r: Shirley, Terry

Saturday 28 August 1954

A year ago I could not have imagined spending a Saturday morning like this. Some of the Dutch boys (including Frits, who's rather taken to Jenny) and their English friend, Tony, are proud possessors of Norton 500cc twin motorbikes, so in between cleaning and dismantling and test-driving them up and down in front of the huts, they chat and flirt with us. Soon, a sports car zooms onto the compound and out gets another of their friends, a tall, dark guy who lives nearby in the Hutt Valley. Anton is French. The moment we're introduced and he says my name, putting the emphasis on the last syllable – Mo-*lly*, I am reminded of Jean-Marie Rousseau, the Frenchman I met in Austria last year. He was partly the cause of my restlessness when we came back to England. Although he wrote the most wonderful "je t'aime" letters for a while and even talked of us meeting up again in the South of France this year, the correspondence tailed off. Anton doesn't have the same romantic appeal, but when he suggests we make up a party and go out for the day tomorrow, I'm very enthusiastic.

Sunday 29 August, 1954

Seven of us gather outside the huts after breakfast on this sunny day. Anton takes it for granted that I'll go in the car with him together with Alma, which leaves Jenny to ride pillion with Frits and Ina with Tony. I am disappointed at having to sit sedately by this man's side when I watch the motorbikes diving and dipping, almost touching the ground as they take the hairpin bends on the Rimutaka mountains. At the summit we pause to take photos and buy ice cream from a tiny kiosk before descending onto the Wairarapa – a vast area of agricultural land, of sheep, of small, dull towns like Masterton and Pahiatua. Although bigger, Palmerston North has a depressing, deadly-hush emptiness about it, reminiscent of Potters Bar on Sundays. But this is *not*

Potters Bar, I remind myself; how dare I make such a comparison! On the way back we stop off at a café which Frits and Tony discovered some time ago. Here we gorge ourselves on sausages, eggs, bacon, beans and tomatoes – such a treat after the ghastly camp food.

As we often do after we've put the lights out, Jenny and I have a heart to heart. She likes Frits a lot and he likes her.

"What about you and Anton? He seems keen."

"Mmm," I mutter, "not *really* my type."

Saturday 11 September 1954

Lots of the girls have now moved into Wellington, including Grace. She is sharing a bedsit with Alma and Ina in Glen Road, Kelburn, a suburb reached by cable car from the city centre. Perversely, I continue to relish the rigours of life at Trentham, even when the rain drums interminably on the tin roofs and turns the grassy patches between the huts into a sea of mud. What I really enjoy is when we pile into someone's room and sit around on the floor or beds, knitting and chatting. Some of the girls have dared to buy heaters, which they keep hidden in wardrobes.

As always, I'm extremely sensitive to the impression that I make on people and in face of Terry's sophistication and Jenny's practical nature there are moments when I feel inadequate. Also, because no-one else seems to get as many letters from home as I do, I try to hide the fact that both Mum and Dad write to me every week.

Monday 13 September 1954

The journey into Wellington every day has become a riotous affair. Chattering, laughing, knitting, sometimes giving voice to the latest number on the hit parade, we shatter the peace and quiet of our fellow passengers. Shirley is usually the last to clamber aboard, often clutching a half-eaten piece of toast. Disapproving looks from local girls and indulgent smiles from some of the men only act as a spur for even more merriment.

As was the case at the BBC, I'm the youngest member of staff and lap up the fuss everyone makes of me. This morning I enjoy a privilege hitherto bestowed exclusively on Hilary – morning coffee with Tom in a milk bar on Lambton Quay. I chat away to him as if he were an old friend.

Anton takes me to the camp cinema tonight. He likes me a lot, but he irritates me – he's so intense. My indifference seems, damn it, only fuel to his passion. Odds are that if I had fallen for him, he wouldn't be so keen.

Wednesday 15 September 1954

I have written an article about the voyage and my first impressions of New Zealand. Yesterday, I managed to type it out while Hilary was at lunch and have just posted it to *The Hatfield and Potters Bar Gazette*.

Awaiting me at Trentham tonight is a letter from Anne, enclosing a photo of the wedding. This took place at St. Augustine's Church, Napier on Saturday 21 August. Noel is a handsome fellow and Anne looks lovely in a low-necked taffeta dress and small crescent-shaped hat. They have gone down to the South Island and are living in a rented flat in Christchurch. She says that both Grace and I will be very welcome to visit next year.

Saturday 18 September 1954

As Jenny sweeps the mats outside the hut and the lads mess about with their motorbikes, Norma, an older friend of Tony's who lives in the Hutt Valley, turns up. She's very jolly and mannish and rather bossy. We take some crazy photos and plans are made for eight of us to go out tomorrow on the motorbikes – Jenny and Frits, the engaged couple Margaret and Roy, Norma and Tony and me riding with Kaess. Anton, thank God, is away this weekend.

Saturday morning clean-up at Trentham –
Jenny on her broomstick

Saturday morning at Trentham –
the Dutch boys, the motorbike and me

Motorbike outing, Sunday 19 September, 1954. Photo of the gang
at the top of Rimutakas, on way to Palmerston North

Sunday 19 September 1954

Can anything be more thrilling? Crash helmets fastened, the bikes revved up, we roar away from the camp in file onto the open road. The wind slapping at my face leaves me almost breathless and as we duck and weave on the Rimutakas, I cling on for dear life. I love every moment though, especially when people turn to stare as we pass in convoy through small towns. I wish we could go further up country, but have to be content again with Palmerston North. At least I'm able to finish my reel of film, taking photos of the Manawatu Bridge, the War Memorial, the fountain and railway line. On the home run, we stop for a slap-up meal at the roadside café we visited before.

Wednesday 22 September 1954

Initially, I'm flattered when Anton invites me round to his home this evening to meet his mother, a dainty, white-haired lady enveloped in a shawl. I even try a little of my 'O' level French on her. Soon, though, things take a strange turn. On her instruction, Anton brings out of a trunk a set of what turn out to be heirloom sheets and other linen, all carefully wrapped in layers of tissue paper. Why *on earth* should I be interested in such things? Then the penny drops – I'm being vetted as a potential daughter-in-law. My hackles rise, but at the same time I want to laugh – it's all so bizarre. Eventually mother retires for the night and Anton kisses me.

"Come and lie on my bed for a bit," he says.

This is not a good idea.

"No, no, *no!*" I whisper as he starts to get exceedingly passionate.

"But I love you Mol-*ly,* I love you."

I push him away and struggle to sit up.

"Please Anton, *stop*! I have to go."

Back at Trentham Jenny's still awake. We exchange gossip and also decide that if we're going to travel once our contract expires, we need to get part-time jobs.

Wednesday 29 September 1954

A restaurant on Lambton Quay wants an evening waitress. Me – *a waitress*? I'm the world's clumsiest…. Nonetheless, I force myself to go along for an interview after work. The Boronia is smallish and intimate, serving soup, meat and two veg, pudding and custard. Jack, the cook, a starved-looking, scraggy-necked Dickens-like character with rasping voice and cough, is fearsome. On the other hand, Connie his wife, with her tired face and grey hair scraped back into a bun is gentle and soft-spoken. The hours are 5-7.30 p.m. Monday to Friday, wages £3 per week.

Wednesday 6 October 1954

It was a scary moment on Monday evening donning overalls and taking my first orders at the Boronia. Now, I'm beginning to enjoy myself. One or two of the customers have been asking where I come from in England and even giving me tips. At the end of the evening I have to set up the tables for the next day and fill the salt and pepper pots, jobs that gives me a peculiar satisfaction. Tonight I'm told that the other waitress, Brenda, whom I have scarcely had a chance to get to know, is leaving on Friday and Jack asks:

"You wouldn't have a friend who'd be interested, would you Molly? I like English girls."

I mention Jenny and rush back to Trentham to tell her the good news.

Sunday 10 October 1954

We're all messing around as usual in front of the huts when Anton arrives. I give him a lukewarm reception, but brighten up when he suggests that we all go to the race meeting at Trentham next Saturday. That will be an exciting experience, one I would never have had at home.

Friday 15 October 1954

Jenny's so efficient and quick in the café – you would think she'd been waitressing all her life. Another thing – when Jack scolds Connie, which happens frequently, I quake, but not Jenny. She's fearless. Tonight we have our first encounter with a customer who habitually comes in just before closing time. He's an unsmiling, fat-bellied eccentric in a Fair Isle pullover, who chomps his way through soup, *two* entrées and *two* desserts, then sits over a cup of tea to the last possible moment.

Saturday 16 October 1954

Intent on looking as glamorous as possible for the race meeting, I spend ages getting ready. I wear my favourite outfit – grey suit, white blouse, tan accessories. Anton goes gooey over me the moment he arrives, but I brush him aside, impatient to get on with the day.

The scene does not disappoint. I even let Anton take charge and show me how to place a modest bet. Sipping gin and tonic and smoking a cigarette in the midst of all this colour and noise, knowing I look my best, I feel like a film star. Once the first race is under way though, it's impossible to maintain my poise. As the horses come thundering round the bend towards us and I see my number taking the lead I start to shriek and jump up and down and wave my arms, and when it streaks past the winning post, I'm ecstatic:

"I've won! I've won!"

Anton disapproves of my exuberance:

"Mo-*lly*, calm down. Calm down."

"Oh, for Christ's sake!"

I push his hand off my arm.

Three races later, sipping another gin and tonic and still flushed with excitement because of my continuing lucky streak, I finally lose my temper with Anton.

"As I'm helping you Mo-*lly*," he whispers, "don't you think we should share the winnings?"

How can such a man who has plenty of money be so mean? I'm flabbergasted. On and on he goes about how I belong to him, et cetera, et cetera. It's just too much. I raise my hand and strike his cheek. His drink spills. I'm aware of a silence around us. All eyes are turned our way. Instantly I regret my impulsiveness.

"I'm sorry, but you drove me to it."

He says nothing, but his face white with anger he turns on his heel and walks off.

Although I feel scared and my conscience pricks, I defiantly stay on with the others to the end of the race meeting.

Back at the camp I wonder what I should do with myself this evening. At dinner I sit with this girl Valerie. She suggests that we go to the dance in the Agricultural Hall in Lower Hutt. It doesn't turn out to be anything special and with the day's events still very much on my mind I'm glad to return to the camp and go to bed. Jenny is not in yet.

At 1.30 a.m. I come to with a start; someone is rapping on the window. I stagger out of bed, noting that Jenny's bed is still empty. I pull aside the curtain. God help me, it's Anton! Panic-stricken, I back away, shaking my head, but he continues to gesture for me to open the window. When I do so, he tells me that this has nothing to do with what happened this afternoon but concerns Jenny, Frits, Norma and Tony. As they wanted to go to the cinema in Wellington, he lent them his car, but they have not returned and he's worried. My insides turn over.

"They must have had an accident," I say. "Have you tried the hospitals?"

"A couple – but now I think I go on the motor bike to search for them."

"I'm coming too."

Far too distraught to think properly or consider whether this is a sensible course of action, I slip a warm jumper and trousers over my pyjamas and jump on the pillion seat.
It's only after we've gone a few hundred yards that I ask why we are doing this. He doesn't answer, just keeps right on till he pulls up outside a police station. Ah, I think, as we dismount and go up the steps, this makes sense. But then after he's given his name at the desk, he's led away and someone else conducts me to another room in which – lo and behold – I find Jenny, Frits, Norma and Tony. I stare at them in bewilderment.

"What's happened? Why are you here? Are you hurt?"

Tony explains that on the way back to Trentham from the cinema, the police stopped them and said that the owner of the car had reported it *stolen*. The terrible thing is, although they've protested their innocence over and over again, the police don't believe them. I've never felt so frightened in all my life. They could end up in prison. And *why* did Anton call me out of bed to tell me he was worried when he knew exactly what had happened? We keep going over everything and the hours drag on.

It is 5 a.m. before anyone approaches. Apparently it has taken all this time for Anton to confess that his car was *not* stolen. He has also told the police that because I'm a friend of these people, he did it to take revenge on me for what happened at the racecourse. We're told we can now leave, but this policeman hasn't quite finished.

"*You,*" he says, pointing his finger at me, "are a very, very silly girl. If you carry on mixing with people like him, you're going to end up dead in a ditch somewhere!"

My throat is tight with tears.

"And you're not travelling back with him to Trentham either. One of these lads can take his motorbike – you ride in the car."

Dear God, what would my ex-school colleagues think of goody-two-shoes Molly Baxter now?

Monday 18 October, 1954

I feel despondent. It's Labour Day next Monday which means a long weekend.

This is a blank for me, but out of the blue comes an invitation. Often at work I have to take something down to the Publicity Studios on the floor below. Here I always have a chat and laugh with Eddie and Bill who are on the photographic/technical side of things. This afternoon I walk in on them discussing plans for a camping trip to Masterton at the weekend with other friends. I show great interest and later in the day when I'm downstairs again, Eddie says:

"If you don't mind being the only girl, we've been wondering if you'd like to come along?"

Although camping doesn't appeal to me, I don't hesitate. In total there'll be five fellows and I shall be riding pillion on Eddie's motorbike.

Saturday 23 October 1954

En route to Masterton, on a quiet stretch of road near Weraroa, Eddie asks me if I'd like to take control of the bike for a bit. *Would I?* We swap places.

"Hold onto me tight," I demand.

Following his instructions I rev up the engine and let out the throttle. I wobble at first, but soon gain confidence. I am in my element – such power at my fingertips, such delight spinning along through the sun-dazzled countryside. I drive about 40 miles, even taking a level crossing in my stride.

"You did very well," says Eddie as he takes the controls again.

I swell with pride.

When we reach the motor camp in Masterton two of the other lads, Kevin and Colin, are in the process of unloading their truck. Almost immediately Bill arrives on his motor bike with Bernie. I watch while they erect the tent in which the six of us will sleep. I know I've nothing to fear from this lot trying anything on with me, but what does horrify me is that they expect me to do the cooking.

Indeed, it's made clear that this is *why* I've been invited. Ye Gods! Little do they know that, apart from occasionally helping Mum make an apple pie or cakes (usually when I was being saintly Beth in Louisa M. Alcott's *Little Women*, a role I alternated with that of madcap Jo, the would-be-writer), I know nothing about culinary matters. Naturally, it doesn't take long for them to find out that their chef is a liability rather than an asset. My chips, hacked out with a none-too-sharp knife, emerge from the pan, heated on the primus stove, as an inedible, burnt mass of weird shapes. Well, at least we have plenty of bread and packets of rice bubbles and a tin opener.

It doesn't take long either before I have to admit to myself that I'm not particularly enjoying this first camping experience, but maybe that's because I feel unusually tired and lethargic. This evening there are fireworks on the campsite, but it's a poor show – just a few Catherine wheels and bangers and sparklers. The lads, however, are in high spirits and take a delight in everything. I'm glad when it's time to snuggle down in the sleeping bag that Eddie has brought along for me.

Sunday 24 October 1954

Today we drive to Masterton aerodrome. As if steering the motorbike yesterday were not enough excitement, I now have the opportunity to take to the skies for a short joyride in a Tiger Moth. Although I'm petrified I refuse to let nerves get the better of me. Donning helmet and goggles I climb into the compartment behind the pilot and command Eddie to take photographs. No sooner do we lift off the ground and start to ascend my stomach turns over and as we dip and drop and circle, I have to keep telling myself that I must not be sick. What a relief to be on terra firm again.

After supper, I know why I've been feeling off-colour: the curse has come early and I've no protection with me. Unable to reveal my predicament to the boys, I'm forced to seek aid from another female on the camping site.

Me in the Tiger Moth ready for a joy-ride at Masterton Aerodrome, Labour Weekend, Sunday 24th October 1954

Monday 25 October 1954

This morning, while dismantling the tent, Eddie, Bernie and Bill discuss which route we should take back to Wellington. I'm overjoyed when they decide to go via Palliser Bay. Cape Palliser, as I can see from the map spread out on the grass, is the southernmost point of the North Island. Oh yes please – anything to get away from vistas of sheep and grass of which I've had quite enough. I used to be like this at home when we were travelling by train en route for holidays in Devon or Cornwall. The rural landscape was pretty, but I tired of it easily and longed for sight of the sea.

Our journey to Palliser Bay is spectacular. Passing through a mountain wilderness, we come upon an uninhabited and desolate landscape of strewn boulders, surf pounding the beach and sea birds whirling above us. This grand finale to the weekend is what I'll remember most.

Friday 29 October 1954

Obviously my failure as a camp cook has not been held against me for here I am invited to spend the weekend at Eddie's home in Eastbourne where he lives with his Mum and Dad and sister Wendy. The house is on the hillside, half-hidden by bush and trees, its verandah cluttered with boots and bikes and garden tools. I'm put into the bedroom, which overlooks Kapiti Island in the middle of the harbour. The family's attitude towards me is casual and relaxed, Eddie and Wendy constantly bickering while we eat a supper of fish and chips. Not for the first time in my life, I'm glad that I don't have brothers and sisters.

After dark the place is spooky and I lie awake a long time, listening to mysterious rustlings from the nearby bushes and trees, my imagination running wild. Roll on the morning.

Saturday 30 October 1954

We're getting ready to go to the Carterton Agricultural Show. This is a major operation because we're travelling in

Eddie's ancient and extremely battered secondhand car, a two-seater Rugby. He spends ages tinkering with the engine and then, when he's satisfied with that, there's the question of where we're going to put the picnic hampers. Eventually he comes up with the bizarre idea of placing them on the running board, threading rope through the strapping, then pulling it up tight and fastening it to the edge of the front window above the steering wheel.

Are we ever going to make it, I ask myself, as the car chugs and groans and makes tinny noises on yet another bend of the Rimutakas. God knows what we would do if we break down here.

This journey proves to be much more exciting than the Agricultural Show itself.

Nothing is as I imagined. There are few people and few sideshows; even the horse-jumping contest lacks excitement. The only real fun comes from my first-ever ride on the dodgems. Even so, Eddie's childish shouts of "got yer!" every time we crash into another car irritates me.

Sunday 31 October 1954

I wake very early as usual. From the window I can see the sea winking diamonds and I long to be outside. Time rolls on and I'm famished. Is anyone ever going to get up? Finally, at noon, we sit down to egg and bacon and sausage and then Eddie and I are off to Days Bay on the motorbike. We sit on the beach for a bit, then go up Ferry Hill and take photos. Time passes amiably enough, but I doubt whether I'll go out with Eddie again.

Saturday 13 November 1954

Another fun Saturday morning at Trentham with Frits, Jenny, Tony, Norma, Kaes and plans are made to go to Wanganui tomorrow on the bikes.

Tonight I go dancing in Lower Hutt with two of the Trentham girls. I decide to wear my navy and white Horrocks cotton sundress because I always have a good time in it. I bought it in Oxford Street one Saturday morning last year. It was way beyond what I'd paid for a dress before, but I liked it so much that I scraped out all the last sixpences and pennies from my purse to make up the £3.9s.11d. What a hoo-ha it caused at home. Mum and Dad were furious that I had spent so much and I stormed up the stairs, sobbing my heart out.

The dress does not fail me tonight. This nice-looking Kiwi, Phil, keeps asking me to dance and I agree to go onto a party with him afterwards. However, as soon as we clamber into the back of a small van along with others and start to snog I feel uneasy. Where will it end? Abruptly I announce:

"I've changed my mind about the party. I want to go back to Trentham please."

Phil tries to persuade me to do otherwise, but I insist I don't feel very well. When the van stops along the Camp Road, he gets out with me.

"No need to come any further," I say.

Suddenly he turns on me and yanks at one of the straps of the sundress, leaving my shoulder bare.

"You Pommy girls," he sneers, "you're all the same."

He strides off back to the van. Scared, I run all the way to our hut. Oh dear, I do seem to get myself into some scrapes.

Sunday 14 November 1954

Shall I ever get over the sense of occasion I feel at being in New Zealand? Even little things excite me – like this morning when a flock of sheep and their drover block the road at Whangaehu. I'm sure the others would think me barmy if they knew how I'm affected by such moments.

Our first sight of Wanganui is looking down on it from the Durie Hill tower. In the foreground is a winding river, houses the other side of it petering to a vista of hilly slopes and bush and trees, which stretch as far as the eye can see. The town itself is quiet and spacious with parks and gardens and fountains. This area was once an important Maori stronghold and I take a photo of the statue of Major Kemp who helped the British in the Maori wars. One of the roads we come upon culminates in Queen's Park Hill, which is crowned with an imposing building – the Sargeant Art Gallery. I wish I could find out more about the history of the place, but we don't have time for that sort of thing. The day ends with our usual feast on the way back to Trentham.

Monday 29 November 1954

I'm overjoyed, but also horror-struck when I get home from work this evening to discover in the postbox the 19th November edition of the *Hatfield and Potters Bar Gazette* which contains my article on New Zealand. Oh, how *could* they give it such a title?

"IF IT'S A MAN YOU WANT, THEN COME ON OUT TO NEW ZEALAND", SAYS MOLLY BAXTER FROM 'DOWN UNDER'.

Can't I just hear all those bitchy Potters Bar girls murmuring – "*Now* we know why she went!" Yes, I did indeed mention the fact that New Zealand overflows with men of different nationalities and girls can take their pick, but that was *not* the reason for writing the article. What does delight me, however, is the *A Girl You Might Envy* editorial column, which goes on about it taking a lot of courage for a young girl to give up her family, et cetera, and ends by wishing me well.

I don't tell anybody here about the article. I remember only too well how embarrassed I was at 14 when one of the Potters Bar boys grabbed the school magazine in which there was a piece about my Cornish holiday and mockingly read it aloud to the rest of our gang.

Monday 6 December 1954

It doesn't seem right wearing summer dresses and sandals while listening to Bing Crosby dreaming of a *White Christmas* and seeing the shops full of snowy-landscaped cards. Also, although this is peak time for the great outdoors and going on holiday, we understand that roast turkey and mince pies form as much part of the New Zealand celebration as in the northern hemisphere.

Presents for England were dispatched by sea mail in October. I sent Mum and Dad a small, round-topped coffee table patterned in different New Zealand woods. I'm sure they'll be thrilled with it because it's so different from anything I could have bought in England.

Everyone seems to have plans made for the festive season. Grace is spending Christmas Day with her flatmates, Ina and Alma and another girl from her office and then goes up to Auckland on Boxing Day for a holiday with Sheila. Shirley, Bettie and Terry, together with Tom and some of the other guys are going into the bush for a couple of weeks. Tonight, much to my relief, I learn that Jenny, Frits, Tony, Linn and lots of others will be on camp and that management is putting on a special Christmas lunch for us. The problem for me is what to do with the rest of the break?

Wednesday 8 December 1954

This morning I pluck up courage and ring Grace to ask if it would be all right if I came to Auckland too. She says yes, but I shall have to find my own accommodation as Sheila has already made arrangements for them. This is no problem. Immediately I ring up the YWCA in Auckland's Queen Street and book a room, then at lunchtime I go down to the station to reserve a seat on the overnight train leaving Wellington late on Boxing Day.

Saturday 25 December 1954

We draw the curtains on an overcast sky and a lifeless Trentham.

"Happy Christmas!"

"And to you Jenny."

How strange everything seems, yet I'm not in the least homesick. We exchange presents. I give her toiletries while she hands me a photo album, the cover of which is handsomely embossed with the painted face of a Maori chief. For breakfast we eat some of the Christmas pudding

Mum sent me in her parcel and wash it down with a glass of beer, then take photos of each other.

Lunch is *awful*. Thin, unappetising slices of turkey, the usual vegetable muck and Christmas pudding served with a great dollop of lumpy custard. What shall we do next, we wonder? With rules on segregating the sexes relaxed for today, Jenny suggests we have a party in our room.

It's amazing how we manage to cram so many into such a small area. We listen to records and dance, laugh, drink, chat. I love every minute. Suddenly though at about six o'clock dear, incorrigible Jenny decides the room is filthy. She tells everyone to get out and come back in half an hour. I protest, but to no avail and have to sit on the bed with my legs curled up under me while she scrubs the floor. We then carry on celebrating until 10 p.m. What a bizarre Christmas Day, but such fun.

Sunday 26 December 1954

I meet up with Grace on Wellington station. Although we're in the same compartment, we're sitting at opposite ends on account of booking at different times. I can hardly contain my excitement at the thought of this 14-hour, 425-mile journey and I'm soon engrossed in the brochure, which details the places of interest we pass through and also maps out the route.

The building of the North Island Main Trunk Railway (opened 1908) is the sort of pioneering accomplishment which stretches my imagination – all those men hacking their way through an impenetrable landscape and even – following upon the Waikato war, – risking violent death at the hands of the Maoris. The steepest part of the climb is the Raurimu Spiral – "a complete circle, three horseshoe bends and two tunnels": we shall see this to advantage on our return journey in daylight.

The railway became news in England last Christmas. The Queen and the Duke of Edinburgh had begun a month-long tour of the Antipodes and naturally I was following their progress avidly. Then came the horrific crash, which happened on the line ten miles south of Okahune, just below Tongariro National Park when Mt. Ruapehu's crater lake suddenly discharged thousands of tons of water. Unsuccessfully, someone tried to warn the train driver not to cross the bridge. Halfway across, the engine and first carriage plunged into the river, to be followed by five other carriages. The sixth coach balanced on the edge while the rest of the train stayed on the bank. 151 died and the Queen awarded medals to some of those who had tried to rescue people trapped in the waterlogged carriages.

Monday 27 December, 1954 – Monday 3 January, 1955

They said in the office that Auckland is more cosmopolitan than Wellington, so I built up images which now I'm here don't match up to the reality. Queen Street, for instance, although it has two large department stores and a post office with an imposing façade, has none of the bustle of Oxford or Regent Streets. However, the YWCA, ideally sited at its top end , is just the sort of place I had expected Trentham to be and is fine for my needs.

Grace and Sheila are staying in a boarding house on the North Shore, so we either meet up in Auckland or I go over to Takapuna on the ferry. Dawn, who is the daughter of their landlady, also accompanies us on our outings. City sightseeing includes a visit to the zoo and the Domain, which is a nature reserve of 200 acres – a lake, lots of trees and bushes and tropical plants, but very humid. Capping the summit, overlooking Devonport and Rangitoto Island, is the War Memorial; there is also a fine museum with marbled floors and lots of Maori artefacts. Outside I'm delighted to find a statue of Robbie Burns, the poet I discovered on that magical Scottish holiday in 1950 and whose ballads I've read time and again.

We also do plenty of swimming and sunbathing, either on the North Shore's Milford Beach, or at the seawater Parnell Baths on Auckland's waterfront. This spacious and dazzling white pool is the best I've ever seen. The pièce de résistance is our trip to Waiheke Island on the Hauraki Gulf – such a poetic name for an island, which I can't help associating with Hawaii (Waikiki) and which I also hope to visit one day. The intensity of emotion I feel as we step onto the ferry for the hour-long journey almost equals that I experienced when we boarded the *Captain Cook*. Each of us is given a brochure about Waiheke, headed up *The Story of the Island*, a fun map on one side and on the other a tongue-in-cheek historical account – for example:

> There have been people on Waiheke Island for a thousand years: But today the old traditions are dying out. The historic habit of eating each other no longer meets with approval although the original settlers considered it pleasant and frugal…….

On a serious note we learn that the Maori name for the island, which is the fifth largest in the New Zealand archipelago, is Te-Motu-Arai-Roa meaning 'The Long Sheltering Island,' and that the population of 2000 people is outnumbered twelve times by sheep.

We disembark at Surfdale wharf and walk the short distance across the island to Pacific Parade and Oneroa – rolling surf, grassy dunes and coconut palms. According to the brochure these palms were imported and planted by New Zealand champion wrestler, 'Lofty' Blomfield and "may some day provide a tropical setting for Oneroa's incomparable beach." We spend the day here sunning and surfing before reluctantly returning to the mainland.

New Year's Eve celebrations are disappointing. I've imagined hundreds of people congregating in Queen Street, strangers talking and dancing together, culminating in one vast linking of hands to sing *Auld Lang Syne* at midnight….. Oh yeah? The reality is that we parade up and down a near empty street while cars filled with lusty young men, hooting and tooting, speed past on their way to private parties. Bored silly, we part company long before midnight.

Tuesday 4 January, 1955

Our train back to Wellington leaves promptly at 8.10 a.m. and what a magnificent scenic journey this proves to be. We travel through mountains, bush and forest via tunnels, major viaducts and bridges, passing over deep gorges and rivers. The most spectacular scenery – the Raurimu Spiral, the volcanic peaks of Tongariro, Ngauruhoe and Ruapehu – lies between Frankton Junction which we reach at 10.30 a.m. and Taihape at 4.45 p.m. Once across the Makohine

Viaduct the landscape pans out to the more familiar farmlands around Feilding and Palmerston North. At 10.20 p.m. we arrive in Wellington.

Wednesday 5 January 1955

What a shock last night to discover that Jenny has moved out of the room and taken one on her own at the other end of the hut. This morning she tells me why: I'm too untidy. Although I feel hurt, I know she's right and in a way it's good to have more room to myself. Jenny also said on the train going into work that she's giving in her notice at the Boronia: she can no longer stand Jack and his overbearing ways. Terry says she's interested in taking her place.

I also learn that Shirley was taken ill with pleurisy in the bush and had to be taken to hospital. What a truly awful thing to happen. She certainly won't forget her first Christmas in New Zealand in a hurry.

Friday 7 January 1955

Grace and I are planning to take advantage of Wellington's long Anniversary weekend to hitch-hike to Napier. I'm so pleased to be getting close to her again because I have always felt guilty about us splitting up when we first arrived.

Saturday 15 January 1955

Jenny, Frits, Tony, Kaes, Linn and me go out on the

motorcycles to Paraparaumu beach. We stay there till late afternoon, basking in the sun and swimming. On return, unable to face the canteen meal, we eat fried eggs and baked beans in the café along the camp road.

Tuesday 18 January 1955

Not only is Terry now at the Boronia, but Shirley has come to do the washing up – great fun. Despite Jack's moods, I still enjoy working there and am very proud of being able to carry three plates in one hand. I love it, too, when customers praise my efficiency, but I never fail to tell them that my *real* job is in an office.

Saturday 22 January 1955

It's such a great feeling to be out on the open road with Grace. With rucksacks on our backs and thumbs poised, we are ready for whoever and whatever. Indeed, any fears we have of not getting lifts or being stranded in the middle of nowhere are instantly dispelled when we're picked up by this Kiwi couple, who take us as far as Levin. They ask us lots of questions about ourselves and boost our confidence by declaring how brave we are. No sooner do we wave them goodbye, then another car stops. This time we get as far as Dannevirke. Here a young man pulls up and – hallelujah – is going all the way to Napier.

We have no difficulty in securing two nights' bed and breakfast at Glasgow House right at the back of the Marine Parade. The landlady is a motherly sort and makes us feel very welcome. Without more ado, we deposit our rucksacks and set off to explore. I've really been looking forward to seeing Napier because I've read quite a bit about it at work – how it suffered a devastating earthquake in 1931 and was rebuilt in Spanish mission style. Also how Alfred Donett, a 19th century literary civil servant, who was a one-time friend of Robert Browning, gave the streets names such as Dickens, Thackeray and Tennyson. This made the town sound so romantic, which, alas, it is not.

The best part is the Marine Parade. Fringed on its ocean side by a narrow beach and on the town side by Norfolk Pines, it stretches as far as the eye can see. Here are all sorts of interesting things and activities – mini-golf, rollerblading rink, sunken gardens and a Sound Shell with a concert platform and the bell of the ship, the *HMS Veronica*. I'm particularly enamoured of the Pania on the Reef statue, which is inspired by the Maori legend of Pania, who fell in love with a mortal and lived on land with him, but was turned to stone when she tried to get back to the sea.

Anniversary Weekend – hitch-hiking trip to Napier with Grace.
Me outside our b & b. Monday 24 January 1955.

Sunday 23 January 1955

After a hearty breakfast of bacon and eggs we take off to West Shore beach where we spend the day sunbathing and swimming and planning a trip to Rotorua in February.

Monday 24 January 1955

Before setting off for Wellington, we take photos of each other outside the guesthouse. Three lads going by pause to whistle.

"What are your names? Where you going? Come for a walk with us," they call out, then start to follow us.

"Let's pretend we're French," I say to Grace.

We gesture and shrug and talk in a mixture of half-remembered words and phrases until they drift away. No problem again with lifts and we're both so enthused with hitch-hiking that we decide this will be our mode of travel to and from Rotorua.

Monday 31 January 1955

After thumbing through brochures in the office, I ring Grace and suggest that because there's so much to see in Rotorua and because we can only afford £6 each for the whole week, we take a blanket with us and sleep under the stars. She agrees. How lucky we are to have all these travel opportunities I muse in bed tonight. Who would credit it – three holidays in less than two months? Sometimes I feel as if I'm living in a dream and I remember all those summer days in Potters Bar, sprawled supine on the lawn, looking up at the sky and determining that one day I would see the world. Now it's coming true.

Saturday 5 February 1955

Our rucksacks are heavy, but getting lifts again proves easy. The only time we feel apprehensive is when we're deposited on the Desert Road at Wairou, an area used by the military for training purposes. While it is not the Sahara, nonetheless the road ahead runs through a desolate landscape of tussock and gravel and is at this particular moment devoid of humanity. We walk a little way, then notice a garage. Surely someone's bound to stop here for petrol and take pity on us? As we approach a young man of slight build and dressed in white overalls appears. He looks us up and down.

"Hi girls, where are you off to?"

"Rotorua."

"Really! Well, that's where I'm going when I've finished my shift. If you like to hang around for a bit, I could give you a lift. I'm Ralph."

We can't believe our luck and as we drive along we chat away about England and the BBC and our future travel plans. I ask him if Rotorua is his hometown. He says, no, but he's got a weekend bach there.

The sky is overcast and as we look out at the bleak landscape of Tongariro National Park, the thought of sleeping in the open has no appeal and I wonder if Grace feels the same way. At Lake Taupo Ralph suggests we stop off for tea. We're ravenous and eat scones and cakes till we're bursting, but Ralph won't hear of us paying for our share. What's more, he asks if we'd like to make a short detour and see the Huka Falls before heading for Rotorua. Yes please! I love waterfalls as much as I do mountains. On the Scottish holiday with Mum and Dad in 1950 I would go into ecstasies when we went out on the lochs and I saw those cascades of water hurtling down hillsides. This, of course, is different, for here we're within yards of the Falls, picturesquely framed by ferns and bracken and tall trees.

It's half-past six when we set off again and it's now that Ralph asks where we plan to sleep tonight.

"Oh," I say with a nonchalance I'm far from feeling, "in a field somewhere. We've got blankets."

"If you like", he says, "you could stay in the bach. I've got one or two friends up there for the weekend, but it can sleep six."

Grace and I exchange glances. I can see she's of my mind.

"Of course we'll pay for our food", I say.

"Oh, we'll sort that out later."

Our relief is short-lived. As dusk comes on and we continue to ride mile after mile through a black wilderness, relieved occasionally by the headlamps of another car, nagging doubts begin to grow and conversation dries up. As if Ralph's reading our thoughts, he tells us that we're nearly there, but still no signs of habitation. Perhaps we're not going to Rotorua. Perhaps…. I berate myself for letting imagination get the better of me, but doubt becomes fear when Ralph slows the car and veers off onto an unlit, rutted track. This leads to a field where there are two wooden huts, one of which is lit up. Ralph parks the car between them.

"Before I show you the living quarters," he says, indicating the darkened hut on the left, "I'll introduce you to the others."

Nothing has prepared us for this. Naked light bulbs shine down on a long wooden table which is strewn with bottles and spilt beer. The stench is overwhelming. Two young men are slouched back in chairs, while a girl, who is well and truly sloshed, lifts her head and greets us –

"Hi yous."

We just about manage a smile before Ralph ushers us over to the other hut. This is furnished with six bunk beds, bathroom and cooking facilities and is at least clean.

"All right?" he asks.

We counterfeit enthusiasm.

"Yes, very good."

"Well, I'll leave you to unpack and freshen up – then when you're ready, come across and join us. Okay?"

Alone for the first time in many hours Grace and I stare at each other, horrified and panic-stricken. What are we going to do? There is only one option – to get the hell out of here and hope that we find someone who can direct us to Rotorua. Hearts thumping, stomachs churning, we position our rucksacks and slowly open the door. From the other hut we can hear the faint sound of music, but just as we make to move off, Grace clamps a hand over her mouth.

"Molly! My camera! I've left it in the car. I can't go without it."

I'm frantic.

"Supposing he's locked it?"

Petrified, I stand guard while she tiptoes out and tries the handle. It gives, thank heaven, but even though she shuts the door quietly, the click sounds loud in the silence and we stand motionless until we're sure that nobody has heard us. Once we hit the track that leads down to the road, we break into a run, not easy with the load on our backs.

Our legs grow weary and we have to keep urging each other on, but the ludicrousness of our situation provokes an outburst of merriment.

"Wait [pant] till he [pant] realises [pant] we're gone," I splutter.

"Oh please Molly [pant], don't [pant] make me [pant] laugh any more."

Out on the road we walk fast and soon come upon a row of houses. Agreeing beforehand what we're going to say – that we're lost and would it be possible to use a 'phone and ring for a taxi to take us into Rotorua – we knock at the first house showing a light. We're in luck; neither husband nor wife ask any questions, but tell us we're not far from the town and oblige our request. Within ten minutes we're on our way, suffering only one last moment of panic when the cab turns and goes past the track leading to the bach. Suppose Ralph is out looking for us?

"Duck" I yell at Grace.

Whatever the driver thinks of us suddenly disappearing from view, he remains unperturbed. Indeed, he proves a lifesaver. He recommends a guesthouse and even waits for us to confirm with the owner that she has a vacancy before driving off. As tired as we are, we keep mulling over what's happened. Although we take delight in picturing Ralph's face when he discovers we've vamoosed, the experience has been sobering. We know we were far too naive and trusting and what a crazy idea, to think we could sleep in a field. The problem now is money. How can we possibly afford to stay in Rotorua for a week if we have to pay for accommodation? Certainly, anyway, we'll have to move to something cheaper tomorrow, but what then?

"Look," says Grace, "I've got £9 in my Post Office

account. If I can arrange to have it transferred up here, we'll be okay."

I'm overjoyed. I know Mum and Dad have always insisted that I never lend money, nor borrow it, but this is an exceptional circumstance and I assure Grace that I'll pay her back as soon as possible.

Sunday 6 February 1955

We have no difficulty in getting a cheaper room in a garden annex of another guesthouse. Provided all goes well at the post office tomorrow, we work out that we shall also be able to afford to do all the tours I've marked off in the brochure. Not wanting to waste a moment we decide to do one of them this afternoon – a bus ride to Whakarewara and tour of the Maori reserve (inclusive price of 3s.8d). In the meantime we walk around the town, which is permeated by the rotten egg smell of sulphur. God help us if we were feeling queasy!

At 2 p.m. we board the bus in Arawa Street, opposite the post office. Soon we disembark and walk towards a white stone arch, headed up with the greeting TEHOKOWHITU-A TU (Welcome to You). On its left flank is a commemorative plaque to those Maoris who fell in the 1914-18 war and on the right another for the victims of 1939-45. A red-ochred fence fans out each side of this arch, punctuated every few yards with a carved head. Immediately inside the archway is a wooden bridge. This spans a steaming pool in which Maori children frolic and dive for the coins people throw down. Beyond the bridge there are huts and silica white ground, pitted and shelved and running with water. Steam spurts out through the cracks, misting the air.

All this goes far beyond what my fertile imagination has conjured up. I'm entranced and even more so when our guide turns out to be none other than the renowned Rangi. Dressed in native costume – woven skirt, flaxen cloak – she has a long, powerful but friendly face.

The area, she warns us at the start, is not without danger and we must obey the rules. We see what she means when we tread the narrow paths that criss-cross this vast, steaming, bush-rimmed plateau of volcanic rock and look down into fiercely boiling pools of water. The most thrilling spectacle of all is the Pohutu Geyser which, exploding into the air, emits great jets of steam and millions of drops of prismatic water. Rangi explains how the natural supply of hot water facilitates cooking. Vegetables, for example, are put into baskets of woven toi-toi grass, which are let down into the steaming holes. Meat can also be done in this way, taking about two hours to cook. One of the native foods is a sweet potato called kumera.

Rangi shows us, too, how the washing is done by dividing one end of a large pool of water into small concrete-edged compartments, each of which is about three feet deep and fitted with taps and plugs. Finally we visit the Maori Pa – a village protected by tall, closely packed palisades, such fortification becoming necessary after the arrival of the first Europeans and firearms. Here also we see the food store – Pataka – which, raised above the ground, is ornately carved and roofed with thatch.

It's a fascinating afternoon and we return to Rotorua in good spirits to find a cheap café for our evening meal.

Monday 7 February 1955

How happy we are to learn that there'll be no problem in getting Grace's money transferred. Now we can settle down and enjoy all the other trips we've earmarked.

This morning we do the Buried Village – Te Wairoa excursion (bus return 5s.6d, launch excursion 3d and toll 1s.6d). The sky is overcast, but this gives an ethereal quality to our drive through the Tikitapu bush to the Green and Blue Lakes.

"This is a bit different from being in London in February!" I say to Grace, as we step into a boat for a short ride on Lake Tarawera.

The guide tells us how on 10 June 1886 the mountain of that name erupted and formed the giant hollowed crater we can see in the middle of it. The waters of the lake were flung 41 ft into the air and the village of Te Wairoa vanished beneath thick layers of grey volcanic ash.

At the entrance to this buried village, we see the remains of an excavated house (Whare). It is supported by V-shaped slats of carved wood, the doorway flanked on one side by a sculpted figure. Alongside is a placard relating how a 110 year-old priest (Tohunga) predicted the disaster a few days before it happened.

Back in Rotorua we have lunch, before setting off again on the 2 o'clock coach trip (5s.6d return) to the Okere Falls, which lie 13 miles north of Lake Rotorua. This is what I love – on the go all the time, constantly seeing new sights, hearing new stories. To get to the Falls we skirt Lake Rotorua, then walk down a track through dark dank foliage to descend Hinemoa's Steps. The excursion ends with an hour-long cruise on Lake Rotoiti, which is bordered by trees and vegetation and little sandy bays.

Hitch-hiking trip to Rotorua with Grace, February 1955. Grace and me with Maori guide by the launch Wynona *on Lake Rotoiti*

Tuesday 8 February 1955

This morning we enjoy the view of Lake Rotorua from the summit of Mount Ngongotaha and a visit to the trout farm at Paradise Springs, but it is a trip we won't forget in a hurry. The problem arises when we stop off for elevenses and eat our way through a plateful of scones, jam and cream. Cream doesn't agree with me at the best of times, so then to sit in the back seat of the coach which descends the 2,554ft in a series of hairpin bends, turns my stomach upside down. How I'm not sick, I shall never know. Grace, too, feels unwell and back in Rotorua we stagger from the coach like a couple of drunks.

For the rest of the day we mooch around the town and explore the town's Government Reserve. This covers a large area of gardens, in part European-styled and formal and in part tropical (rather like the Domain in Auckland). Here, too, are the usual park facilities – golf and tennis – but central to all is a mock-Tudor building, which contains a complex of remedial, warm-water mineral baths.

At 8 p.m. we make our way to the Municipal Concert Chamber where we've booked to see a display of Maori dancing and singing. This is exciting stuff with lots of whirling and twirling of sticks and pois and shaking of reed-skirted hips. Then comes the Haka, a stirring war dance, which has bare-chested, spear-wielding men rolling their eyes, sticking out tongues and jumping up and down. There's also the rhythmic 'canoe' dance, performed by the women and girls. This relives the story of the journey the Maoris made from Hawaiki to New Zealand (Aotearoa). Paddles sweep an imaginary ocean, pause a moment as the rowers grow weary, then in sight of land start up with renewed urgency. The finale is a rendering of *Now is the Hour* (Poto Ata Rau).

Wednesday 9 February 1955

We still can't get used to the smell of sulphur which on this morning's excursion to Tikitere is even more pungent. In fact, entering this vast 25 acre geothermal field is like entering upon a fantastical, devilled landscape. This great expanse of white-rocked terrain, is pocketed with boiling pools (the temperature, the Maori guide tells us, reaching $600^{\circ}F$) and seething gaseous mud flats, little pockets of which rise and plop, just like eggs frying. All of this is shrouded in vaporous clouds and back-dropped with trees and shrubs. The mud-pools and steam-holes bear dramatic names such as Satan's Glory, Hell's Gate, the Devil's Frying Pan and Satan's Claret Cup.

"Watch this," says the guide and places a penny in the hot sand.

When he takes it out, it has turned silver.

No less interesting, but more tranquil is our afternoon boat trip on Lake Rotorua and a visit to Mokoia Island in the centre of it. On the island we gather round our Maori guide to hear the legend of its inhabitant, Tutanekai, who fell in love with the shore-bound Hinemoa. Her parents disapproved of the match, but she escaped from them by swimming across the lake to the island, where she lived happily ever after with Tutanekai.

As we do most evenings, we find the cheapest meal possible, then walk around the town and retire to our room where we chat for ages.

Thursday 10 February 1955

This is our last opportunity to 'take the waters' so we head for the Blue Baths, the large open-air pool for adults in the Government Reserve complex. The water is warm, the sun hot and we spend an hour jumping in and swimming up and down. While we're dressing though, we begin to feel most peculiar, sort of light-headed and terribly tired. It's only then we realise that a mineral bath is not meant to be used as an ordinary swimming pool: rather it is for relaxing and drifting along gently on one's back. We have learnt our lesson too late and must suffer.

Nonetheless, we manage to scoop up some of Rotorua's therapeutic mud to take back to the guesthouse. At the moment when our faces are caked in a hard green mask and we can barely move our lips, the landlady knocks at the door. She wants her money and to know what time we'll be leaving tomorrow.

Rotorua, February 1955 'Hell's Gate', Tikitere – steam rising from boiling pools can reach temperature of 600 degrees F.

Rotura, February 1955. Grace at entrance to Government Reserve Gardens

Friday 11 February 1955

Hitching back to Wellington today is even more good fun than hitherto. Apart from routine car rides, we're picked up in the Wairarapa region by a farmer towing an empty truck designed to transport sheep, not humans.

"No room for yous in the cab," he says, "but if you want to jump into the truck….."

We wish we could travel all the way back to Wellington like this, but we're dropped off at Levin. The next guy to stop is also a farmer, this time trailing a horse-box; he's old, lots of lines on his face, but very chatty and when he suggests we stop for a cup of tea, we have no qualms in taking up the offer.

Friday 18 February 1955

Tonight, I resign from my job at the Boronia. While I was in Rotorua Terry had the most almighty row with Henry and walked out and Shirley has also left. This has made him even more bad-tempered and I feel I, too, have had enough. However, it's imperative I get another part-time job soon.

Monday 21 February 1955

I'm feeling a bit down in the dumps. Everyone but me has a boyfriend. Jenny continues steadfast with Frits as do Scottish Bettie with Eddie and Linn with her Scotsman, John. Shirley has Sepp, an Austrian and Grace has had a couple of dates with Geurt, the Dutchman she met at the Empress Ballroom. Things also look promising for Terry. Mick works as a chef for the New Zealand Shipping Line, but, of course, this means that he's away at sea for three months at a time. While I still shudder at the thought of settling down, I would love to meet someone special.

Wednesday 23 February 1955

My spirits soar after an interview this evening for a waitressing job at Garland's in Featherston Street, just round the corner from my office. This restaurant serves things like steak, sausages, fish and mixed grills. It's run by a Greek family under the patriarchy of one known as the 'Old Man.' His daughter Maria supervises and helps out where necessary while Theo, his son-in-law, a big jolly man, does the cooking. Hours and wages are the same as at the Boronia and I start on Monday.

Sunday 27 February 1955

Terry and I are at a loose end this afternoon.

"What about hitching a ride somewhere?" she suggests.

"Just as long as we don't get stranded......"

"Oh we won't, I'm sure."

She proves right and we spend an agreeable three hours or so getting to Featherston and back. One lift follows another and always there's the same friendliness and curiosity – questions about where we're from, our opinion of New Zealand, et cetera, et cetera.

Friday 4 March 1955

Following receipt of a letter last night from Anne and Noel in Christchurch and an invitation to go down there for Easter, I ring Grace. She won't be coming, I suppose because of Geurt, but this does not deter me. I relish the thought of another great experience, not least because I'll be at sea again, travelling overnight on the ferry from Wellington to Lyttelton.

Monday 7 March 1955

A week into working at Garland's and Terry has joined me. The other waitress is a Kiwi called Deborah. We look after about six to eight tables each and have to carry orders in our heads. These can get very complicated with all the variations; for example, mixed grill without the sausage; steak with mushrooms and/or onions/tomatoes. Thank goodness I have a good memory, but it makes me realise how hard and unrewarding it is to serve the public, the majority of people seeming oblivious to the fact that waitresses only have one pair of hands.

Wednesday 9 March 1955

Just recently Laurie, who hails from Northern Ireland and is one of the most lively and cheerful guys at Trentham, has been conducting a playful flirtation with me.

"Molly m'darlin', you're looking beautiful as ever," he'll say when our paths cross.

Sometimes he gives me a hug. I haven't thought anything of these exchanges, but tonight in the lounge he asks me whether I'd like to go with him to the dance at the Horticultural Hall in Lower Hutt on Saturday.

Saturday 12 March 1955

I spend a long time getting ready for my date. Laurie is complimentary and very attentive, bringing me soft drinks in between dances and taking me into supper. As we close together for the Last Waltz I feel all stirred up and have no objection when back at Trentham he leads me down the side of the race-course, where we find a niche under a hedge. For the next hour or so I'm transported while we pet and kiss passionately. What's so nice is that he doesn't try to go all the way.

Wednesday 16 March 1955

Inevitably, some of my special friends are talking about moving into Wellington before the winter sets in. While I'm as fed up with the food and conditions here as anyone else, I feel anxious about us all splitting up and, of course, I shall be leaving Laurie behind.

Monday 28 March 1955

Theo announced last week at Garland's that he needs someone to wash up and so much to our delight, Shirley is again working alongside us. As we did at the Boronia the three of us have lots of fun. Theo enjoys flirting with us and telling risky jokes. Sometimes I don't always get them, but laugh heartily anyway. I'm sure he knows I'm still a virgin.

The place is very popular and we do work terribly hard. Friday nights are the worst with often a queue stretching down the stairs. Sometimes tempers fray.

"Where's my order of whitebait?"

"How much longer will the steak and onions be?"

Last Friday Deborah and I had a tug of war with a plate.

"It's mine," I shrieked.

"No it's not. I ordered first."

"Girls, girls, girls – enough." Maria said.

The best part is when Terry and I go along to the post office on Mondays to deposit our earnings in a savings account. We talk endlessly about future travel plans and seek information from shipping companies as new ideas take hold.

Tuesday 5 April 1955

Tonight Larry presents me with a huge gift box tied with red ribbon. Everyone oohs and aahs as I unwrap it and reveal a very large Easter egg, surrounded by chocolates. I'm speechless. While we're snogging in the bicycle shed, he says he wishes I wasn't going to Christchurch tomorrow.

Thursday 7 April 1955

It's so exciting to be at the dockside again, to walk up the gangplank onto the deck, to be part of the buzz and bustle of departure, to breathe in that very special ship's smell. I'm sharing a cabin with a Kiwi girl, Ruth, who is going down south to her family. As soon as pleasantries have been exchanged, I'm up on deck to watch departure and to relive those moments when we sailed through the Heads eight months ago. What a lot has happened since. Still in nostalgic mood I have supper. In bed, rocked gently by the swell of the sea, listening to the familiar creaking and rustling, I long for the day when I shall be embarking on a long voyage again.

Good Friday, 8 April 1955

After a good sleep and hearty breakfast, I bound eagerly up the stairs to see us arrive in the Port of Lyttelton, but I am not impressed. Waiting for the train to take me to Christchurch, I begin to feel nervous at the thought of being with Anne in this totally different environment and of meeting Noel. However, apprehension vanishes the moment I see them at the station and we get into a taxi. There's so much to catch up on, not only what we have been doing for the last nine months, but news of our ex-BBC chums, which comes to Anne via Joyce's letters: Doris is married, Pat has left, et cetera, et cetera.

I immediately feel at home in their flat, but what I find strange is Anne's enthusiasm for domesticity, giving a seal of approval to everything I detest, yet still retaining her sophistication. For example, she's so proud of the matching curtains and cushion covers she made and enjoys cooking.

Visiting Anne (ex-BBC colleague) in Christchurch, South Island Easter 1955 – me sitting with her on the bank of the Avon river.

Easter Saturday 9 April 1955

Today we explore Christchurch of which my expectations had not been high.

Everyone at work told me that it's the most English of all New Zealand cities. Still, it's another new experience, albeit of a more sedate kind than lately encountered and I enjoy walking round the square and the cathedral and sitting for a while on the banks of the Avon.

Easter Sunday, 10 April 1955

As usual I wake up far too early, but read until Noel brings me a cup of tea. Sunday dinner is a real treat after Trentham's dismal Sunday fare and I savour every mouthful of scrumptious roast lamb and homemade apple pie. Afterwards we drive up the Summit Road, through the Cashmere Hills. From the top there's a view of Lyttelton

Harbour and Christchurch – flat and uninspiring – give me Wellington any day. On the way down we stop off for tea and scones in a small, English-styled café.

Easter Monday 11 April 1955

"You'll come again, won't you?" says Anne when we part company "and tell Grace she'd be very welcome, too."

I wonder if I shall return. It's been fabulous seeing Anne again and getting to know Noel, but the visit has left me all churned up inside. Seeing them so much in love and happy to do simple, mundane tasks together has stirred me to the depths, even made me feel closer to Laurie. Yet I'm uneasy, too. As much as I need love and affection, I know in my heart of hearts that he's *not* the one for me. Oh dear how complicated life seems at times.

Thursday 14 April 1955

I have such an embarrassing experience this evening. Not uncommonly, it results from my impatience and eagerness to get on with life. Laurie meets me at Garland's at 7.30 p.m. We haven't gone far when I want to go to the toilet. Luckily there's a big public one en route to the cinema. Still in a tearing hurry, I fail to hitch up my skirt properly, the consequence of which is one large and conspicuous damp patch. I'm frantic and appeal to the attendant.

"I can't go outside like this – my boyfriend's waiting."

To my astonishment and without more ado, she tells me

to take it off, produces an ironing board and presses the skirt dry.

"Gee," says Laurie, "you've been a helluva time."

If only he knew.

Saturday 7 May 1955

Tonight after the dance in Lower Hutt when we're snogging as usual under the racecourse hedge, Laurie asks me to marry him. It's very romantic here under the stars and everything is so perfect at this particular moment that I cannot possibly refuse. We talk for ages and plan to make it official with a ring on my birthday on the 18th.

Sunday 8 May 1955

As soon as I wake up and realise the enormity of what happened last night doubts start to creep into my mind. Although we didn't discuss this, I know Laurie wants to settle down in New Zealand, so what about all my plans to travel once the contract expires? On the other hand, are they ever going to come to fruition? Let's face it, all the girls have regular fellows now and marriage is surely on the cards for them and it would be wonderful not to have to worry any more about losing my virginity.

Everyone's delighted for me.

"Dear Molly, I hope you'll be very happy," Jenny says, hugging me.

"You're made for each other," declares Linn.

"Fantastic news," Bettie shouts.

Yes, I *am* doing the right thing. After lunch Laurie and I go for a walk into the hills immediately at the back of the camp. He has never felt so happy, he says.

Monday 9 May 1955

Screams of delight from the girls at work, but I could do without Ron, who's always so grandfatherly and protective of my welfare, sounding caution:

"Are you sure he's the right one for you, Molly? You haven't known him very long."

How *dare* he question my judgement. I am also irritated by others who rattle on about buying a section and building a house, et cetera.

"Good heavens," I say, "we're not thinking about that yet."

With no work in the in-tray, I type a letter to Mum and Dad. I wonder what their reaction will be?

Monday 16 May 1955

The more I've thought about things this week, the more I've come to realise this engagement is all wrong. However, as much as I hate living a lie, I know I have to go along with it for the time being. Later on I shall have to think up some way to extricate myself.

Wednesday 18 May 1955

Everyone at work admires the engagement ring and makes a

fuss of me on this my 20th birthday. I feel such a fraud though when birthday gifts of the 'bottom drawer' type appear on my desk. While I like the idea of our engagement being announced at the dance at the Agricultural Hall on Saturday, the implications of what I have set in motion are frightening.

Saturday 21 May 1955

My moment of glory arrives, the crowd hushing as the MC takes centre stage.

"Tonight," he says, "we are celebrating the engagement of a couple who've become very popular at these dances – ladies and gentlemen I give you – Molly and Laurie."

A broad smile masks my guilt, but at the same time I can't help being flattered by the applause and all these familiar and unfamiliar faces offering congratulations. This is the sort of attention I've always dreamt of, but when we get back to Trentham and Laurie starts talking about getting married soon, I'm back in the real world.

"Oh not yet," I say, "perhaps next year?"

God forgive me!

Monday 6 June 1955

Finding a flat in Wellington has become the most pressing topic of conversation amongst us Trentham diehards. Reluctant at first, I know moving on is inevitable. An added advantage is that it will offer me an escape route from Laurie. The question is – do I really want to live on my own, and if not, with whom can I share? All this has been going round and round in my mind lately. Then, today, in talking to Grace on the telephone, she says she's fed up with her room in Khandallah. This leads on to the suggestion that we might find a place together and we agree to keep our eyes open for something suitable.

Saturday 11 June 1955

This morning Grace and I look at a bedsit in Hawker Street, just off Courtenay Place at the top end of town. No. 4 is a large house at the bottom of the hill. Steep steps lead up to the front door. Inside there is a room each side of the hallway, but the main living area is on the next floor. Here are six more bedsits, a communal bathroom and large kitchen in which there are half-a-dozen gas rings, cooker with an oven and a copper like Mum has for boiling up clothes. The backdoor leads out onto a yard (where we can peg out) and to another smaller building in which the landlady lives. Each room has two single beds, table, chairs, cupboards and wardrobe. Not the least of advantages is its convenient situation – just a walk or a short tram ride to Lambton Quay. We decide on the spot to take the room and move in next Saturday.

Wednesday 15 June 1955

Now the decision has been taken, I can't wait to get away from Trentham. Everyone else, too, except Linn, who marries John later this summer in Lower Hutt, is on the move or in the process of negotiations. Terry has got herself a bedsit in Tinakori Road; this is up from the railway station past the government buildings. Shirley will be living in Kelburn and, coincidentally, Jenny has taken a room at the top of Hawker Street.

"Gosh, I'm going to miss you," Laurie says dolefully as we kiss goodnight after the pictures.

"But I'll be seeing you at weekends, either here or in Wellington."

"And I shall come up sometimes during the week."

For how long, I wonder?

Saturday 25 June 1955

I adore living in town, the feeling of being at the heart of things. I know this is how it could have been if Mum and Dad had let me get a bedsit in London. Of course, in Wellington there's the added advantage of proximity to my other great passion – the sea. Nothing stirs my imagination more than this wonderful harbour with its stage-setting range of hills and the great ships of the world coming and going all the time – a sight to make me drool with desire to be aboard and sailing off to God-knows-where. In May a new one-class ship, the *Southern Cross*, on its first round-the-world voyage, anchored here and oh how I envied those who were on it.

Then, too, there's a super bunch of girls living at No. 4 Hawker Street, including two Maoris. We have a good old chat and laugh when we meet up in the kitchen at weekends to cook our bits and pieces or to do the washing.

This afternoon Grace and I explore the immediate vicinity and take photos so that we can give our families some idea of where we're living. Even standing on the top of our steps, we can see the hills encircling Wellington and there's a great view of the harbour from the top of Hawker Street where there's a large monastery. Down below is Oriental Bay – such a pretty spot with its pine-backed sandy beach and moored boats.

Laurie comes to town this evening to take me to the cinema. I am pleased to see him, but not so happy when the conversation takes a 'when we are married' turn. I am relieved that we have distance between us, although I continue to worry about how the matter is to be resolved.

Grace outside our new home at No. 4 Hawker Street,
Wellington – June 1955.

Monday 27 June 1955

Dreadful news from home for Grace: James, her younger brother, is suffering from cancer. I feel so useless. What can

I say to comfort her? Thank God she has her Catholic faith and Geurt to lean on.

Tuesday 5 July 1955

James is dead. How can anyone as young as this be struck down in such a horrible way? I can't bear to think about it. I feel much more aware of the significance of death than I did when my grandmother, who lived with my aunts in the next road to us, died in 1944. I remember coming home from school and finding the curtains drawn, but her passing was not talked about in front of me and I stayed with Janet up the road while Mum attended the funeral. Of course grandma was old and remote from me while James had only lived for 18 years. Sad days then for Grace, especially as she is so far from home and cannot share her grief with any of the family. A letter from my Mum and Dad, who keep in touch with Grace's sisters, also expresses their sorrow.

Monday 11 July 1955

At work I'm chatting to Sylvia in the corridor when Hilary sticks her head out of the door.

"Molly, there's a call for you."

The male voice at the other end sounds vaguely familiar.

"Don't you know who it is then….. Brian….. *Captain Cook*?"

I can hardly speak.

"Are you still there?"

"Yes – yes – but where are you calling from?"

He's in Wellington. Having broken his contract and paid back the passage money, he's en route to Australia to see how things are there. He asks if we can have a drink this evening and arranges to meet me outside Garland's at 7.30. Not only am I very excited at the thought of seeing him again, but it dawns on me that I can use this as an excuse to disengage myself from Laurie. All day my stomach is in turmoil and even when we're walking along the road hand in hand I feel nervous. As we take our seats in the Royal Oak hotel bar, I unburden myself about Laurie.

"I can't go through with it," I say, "he's definitely not the one for me."

Brian seems quite unconcerned about the situation. He walks me back to Hawker Street, kisses me passionately and avows to telephone when he gets back from Australia.

Tuesday 12 July 1955

I haven't slept a wink worrying about what I'm going to tell Laurie. At work I wait till I'm alone in the office to ring him, then when he answers I'm so much on edge and so determined to make sure he understands I can't marry him that I babble incoherently.

"Hey, hey, hold on a minute Molly," he says when I finally let him speak, "let me get this straight – all you did last night was have a drink with this fellow you met on the ship coming out to New Zealand?"

"Yes, but…"

"Well I can't see what you've done wrong."

"Oh, but it's much more complicated than that," I insist, "and whatever you say, I just *can't* marry you."

He says he'll come to Wellington this evening and meet me after I've finished at Garland's, so once again I am sick with nerves. This is not going to be easy, but at least it will mean no longer having to live a lie.

We head for Mt. Victoria. It's such a beautiful view from here at night with all the lights cascading down the hillsides, but this is too critical a moment for proper appreciation. Over and over again Laurie says it doesn't matter about Brian; he still loves me, wants to marry me, so *why* don't I want to marry him? All I can stress is that, regardless of Brian, I've changed my mind. I don't want to settle down. I hate seeing him so distressed, but if I relent now, I'm trapped for life.

"Please Laurie," I plead, "just go back to Trentham and forget me. You'll meet someone far nicer than me, really you will."

I take off the ring and hand it to him. He flings it on the ground. I walk away. Please God, I never have to go through something like this again. All I want to do is to crawl into bed and forget that any of it ever happened.

Wednesday 13 July 1955

Grace agrees that I have done the right thing about Laurie and while I'm edgy about telling them at work, they all say it is much better to realise my mistake now rather than later.

"What could be worse than discovering you've married the wrong man?" Tom commiserates over morning coffee in the milk-bar.

I ring Shirley and Jenny and Terry and tell them at Garland's and by the end of the day feel far less guilty about everything.

Sunday 17 July 1955

I'm in one of those self-critical, 'what's life all about?' moods. How *stupid* I was to let my romantic, impulsive nature get the better of me and agree to marry Laurie without giving the matter proper thought. The other girls wouldn't behave like this, I'm sure. Nonetheless, it's not easy being unattached again, especially on a Sunday.

I go to Jenny's place after lunch. Frits and Tony and some of the Dutch boys are there. A couple of them have joined the New Settlers' Club. It sounds just what I need at the moment – social evenings, dances, outings.

Wednesday 20 July 1955

I join the club and feel very daring in putting my name down to go on a skiing trip in August. Imagine me *skiing*! At home this is a sport exclusively for the rich and famous. I go to sleep dreaming of gliding effortlessly down pristine white slopes beneath a deep blue sky.

Saturday 23 July 1955

I'm on tenterhooks all morning and very excited. Brian returned from Sydney yesterday and is coming to Hawker Street this afternoon. We'll be alone as Grace is going over to Geurt's sister for the day. At 2 o'clock he arrives and presents me with a large toy koala bear. I'm thrilled to bits.

"I've broken off my engagement," I rush to tell him. "It was awful, he was so upset, but I just had to do it….."

Again he has nothing much to say about the matter and soon we're engaged in a serious snogging session. Inevitably I have to restrain him and he's unhappy.

"You're not telling me that you're *still* a virgin, Molly?"

Oh dear, why did he have to say that? It spoils everything.

"Well, I'm not the only one," I retort.

We carry on snogging but I feel ashamed, humiliated and resentful. He's going back to Auckland tonight, says he's not sure about his future plans. I *know* I shall never see him again and feel terribly depressed when we say goodbye. Although nothing would persuade me to chance getting pregnant, this virginity issue really gets me down.

Sunday 31 July 1955

In a restless, discontented Potters Bar Sunday mood, made worse by the sun shining and the thought of being on my own all day, I ponder on whether I could possibly go down to Trentham after lunch and say hello to the few remaining people I know there. Well – is that my *real* reason? Isn't it rather that it would be nice to see Laurie again? But is that being fair to him? Nonetheless, some little devil urges me to make the trip and I make myself look as attractive as possible. There's not a soul in sight as I walk the short distance from the station, but the camp lounge is packed.

"Oh, look who's here," someone says.

"Hi Molly, how's it all going?"

And so on and so on until Laurie, who has been engaged in animated conversation with a neighbour, becomes aware of my presence. His face expresses fear, dismay and delight as he extricates himself from the company and comes over to me.

"What are *you* doing here?"

With feigned nonchalance I tell him I just wanted to say hello to everyone. He suggests a walk. We go beyond the camp perimeter towards the edge of the hills. I try to keep the conversation general, stressing how much I love living in town, but when he puts his arm round me and kisses me, I can't resist and we indulge in a long, passionate snog. He thinks of me every minute of every day, he says. Couldn't I possibly change my mind and come back to him? As much as I'm enjoying the physical contact, I force myself to break away.

"Laurie – I can't – I'm sorry, really I am."

His face crumples. Now I can't wait to get back to Wellington.

Tuesday 2 August 1955

Today arrives the usual weekly letter from Dad and I am *livid* – not with him – but with Laurie. He wrote to my parents ten or so days ago, imploring them to persuade me to change my mind. What right had he to do that? However, good old Dad has handled the matter just as I would have hoped. He wrote back and said that he and Mum couldn't possibly make decisions for me and that they were sure I had sense enough to know what I was doing. Why didn't Laurie mention this on Sunday? In white hot fury I write to him as soon as I get home from Garland's, telling him that he should not have involved my parents, et cetera. I soften things a bit by saying how much I enjoyed seeing him again last Sunday, but he must understand that I'm too young to get married.

Friday 5 – Sunday 7 August 1955

This skiing lark doesn't turn out anything like I'd imagined. At first the rough and ready nature of travelling to Mt. Ruapehu on Friday afternoon in one of two large vans and sleeping in it appeals to my sense of adventure. I'm with a great bunch of girls – Ellen, Margaret, Lois, Vera, Frances, Phyllis – and we have great fun on the journey swapping stories and singing. However, it's quite a different matter when I wake cold and cramped at 3 a.m. and find water dripping down my neck.

We are to eat all our meals in a nearby café and after breakfast I feel much better and look forward to the skiing. Ha! Ha! What I haven't bargained for is the icy cold, the rain and the mist and having to grapple with attaching the skis to boots. For a start, how on earth does anyone manage to walk on the snow? Some of the girls are not doing too badly, but I'm hopeless. Moreover, done up in layers of jumpers under my anorak, a peaked, scalp-itching hat crammed on my head, I feel very constricted. At last though in a position to try the gentlest of declines I panic and end up on my back, bottom in the air and one ski, which obviously I had not fastened properly, flying into the air. After that I give up.

The second night in the van is much better than the first and after a morning walk on the lower slopes of Ruapehu – this time in sunshine – we set off for Wellington. Although I do not wish to repeat the experience, I am in high spirits.

Tuesday 9 August 1955

Ye Gods! Will the Laurie saga ever end? Today there's a five-page letter from him in reply to mine, which, he says, he was surprised to receive. He now realises he's lost me for ever, but declares that I shall be very lucky to find someone to love me as much as he did. At least, he goes on, he's going out again and has been to a couple of parties. He also tells me that he can't fathom me out. Well, that's not surprising, given the fact that I can't either. Yet he touches a nerve for he rightly deduces that I love being in town during the week, but feel lonely at weekends.

Monday 22 August 1955

I'm panic-stricken at work today when I'm instructed to go downstairs and relieve on the telephone switchboard for an hour as they are short-staffed. Hopeless at anything technical, I would give anything not to have to put myself through this stomach-turning ordeal. After a quick lesson from Jane, learning how to connect and put calls through, I'm left on my own. And what happens? I cut off at least two people, one of whom would be Mr. Scully. The joy I feel when Jane returns from lunch is inexpressible, but that is not the end of my woes. Talking to her for a bit about boyfriends before returning upstairs, Mr. Williams suddenly appears to tell me that I've left the intercom on.

"Everyone in the building can hear what you're saying Molly."

Although he has a twinkle in his eye, I feel terribly embarrassed.

Last week, too, I made another stupid error. The new bloke in the office, Derek, had given me some shorthand notes. One of the items was the caption for a picture of a large flock of sheep on the Canterbury Plains with drovers enjoying an afternoon tea break. When I took the finished work back to him, he pointed out that I had typed "afternoon *sea* breaks on the Canterbury Plains." How careless of me.

This afternoon Hilary tells me she's leaving. I'm filled with dread at the thought of who might take her place. I shall miss her. She's been my shield and never minded working late when an urgent job has come up and I have had to rush off to Garland's.

Monday 5 September 1955

Our second year of residence in New Zealand has begun. Even if nothing particularly exciting has happened for a while, I'm enjoying the social life offered by the New Settlers' Club.

On Saturday evenings a crowd of us go to the Empress Ballroom in Ghuznee Street. Much larger and a more sophisticated dance venue than those in the Hutt Valley, it attracts plenty of brylcreemed, winkle-pickered and velvet collar types – the sort who never ask me to dance. Of course, I know that's because I lack sophistication. Even when I dance with ordinary-looking blokes I still get nervous. A lot depends on the partner; sometimes I glide effortlessly over the floor, at others I wrong-foot and get in a tangle, ending up embarrassed and apologetic. Inevitably, there are Potters Bar moments – the anxious eyeing of the group of males by the door and pretending not to be disappointed if no-one notices me. What I do enjoy is jiving with the girls in a space at the side of the hall – or, I should say, my particular version of jive, because I've never learnt to do it properly.

Monday 12 September 1955

Hilary's replacement, Gillian (a New Zealander), has been in the office a week. She's pleasant enough, but on the quiet side. God knows what she makes of me, especially when I ring Terry. Terry's office is on The Terrace and this means that we can see each other from our respective windows, so we do a lot of waving and laughing and shrieking.

Photos come in the post today of Mum and Dad's holiday in Alassio, Italy – their first trip abroad. I love the one of them on the beach posing with a group of young Italians and Greeks who apparently became very fond of them. Dad, usually so reserved and unfriendly, is looking happy and cheerful. Oh how it makes me long to go to Italy too.

I also have a letter from Janet, the only Potters Bar friend with whom I keep in touch. Long before the idea of going to New Zealand occurred, she and I talked of going to Canada. Now she informs me she's engaged. The news makes me feel even more on the shelf than before.

Friday 23 September 1955

I've known for a couple of weeks about the New Settlers' plans to spend the Labour Holiday weekend (22-24

October) in New Plymouth, but namely because of finances have dithered about booking. Tonight, when my new friend Dorothy and I make up our minds to go, the organiser tells us that all places are taken. However, he says, if we care to make our own way up there and find accommodation, we can go on the excursions and participate in the entertainment.

"What do you think about hitch-hiking, Dorothy?" I suggest. "I've done it lots of times – great fun and won't cost us anything."

She's enthusiastic and my spirits soar. I can't wait to be on the road again.

Thursday 6 October 1955

Recently a well-spoken, rather formal young man, John, a student at Wellington University, has been frequenting my table in Garland's and in quiet moments I've told him quite a bit about myself – my day job here and working for the BBC at home. He seems a bit shy, but I sense he likes me and wouldn't be surprised if he gets round to asking me out eventually.

Saturday 8 October 1955

Has a fairy godmother at last taken pity on this Cinderella? Tonight at the Empress Ballroom I meet Andrew, who dances several times with me. He's outgoing and jolly, but I have to confess the main attraction lies in the fact that he's an officer on one of the ships currently at anchor in the harbour. He walks me back to Hawker Street and after we've snogged for a bit asks if he can see me when he returns from his next trip up the coast.

Saturday 15 October 1955

Blow me down, if tonight at the Empress I don't meet yet *another* potential boyfriend. Jorgen is Danish, which makes him even more attractive. We dance together the whole evening and he says he'll ring me sometime. My goodness, what will Gillian say if all three of my prospective beaux keep their promise? This male attention has put me back on top of the world.

Saturday 22 October 1955

Dorothy and I set off for New Plymouth at 8 a.m. Within ten minutes of being on the road we're picked up by the first of four benefactors. One ride takes place in a *dust cart*, which greatly amuses us. In marked contrast to this, a young man driving a Zephyr, which even has a radio in it, stops for us at Foxton. He, too, is going to New Plymouth. Unfortunately cloud is thickening as we near the coast, but we get a glimpse of the majestic, snow-capped peak of the 8,262 ft high Mt Egmont (also known as Mt Taranaki) before it is engulfed in mist. By the time we're dropped off in the main street of New Plymouth the rain is teeming down.

Finding accommodation is a matter of urgency, but so is eating. We ferret around in our rucksacks for the sandwiches we brought with us. They're stale, so we succumb to buying paper-wrapped fish and chips which we eat as we go along in search of somewhere to stay – not an easy task, this being a holiday weekend, but at two hotels staff tell us that if all else fails we're to come back and they'll fix something up for us. However, we get a room at a guesthouse called The Chimes, 17s.6d per night, prepare our own breakfast.

Now the whole point of the New Settlers coming to New Plymouth is to be guests of the town's overseas club. Dorothy and I are under the impression that there is a dance tonight on the club's premises, so after changing and having supper in town, we go along there. This is not the case. When we open the door we see only a few people playing table tennis. A young man comes over.

"Nothing on tonight girls," he says, "but if you want to dance, there's one at the Agricultural Hall."

Because the rain is bucketing down yet again, he calls a taxi for us. No wonder the driver is surprised when we tell him our destination for it is only yards down the road.

"Go on," he says when we tender the fare, "keep your money."

What a friendly town this is. We have a couple of dances each and return to the guesthouse at half-past midnight.

Sunday 23 October 1955

Today we join up with the New Settlers and the New Plymouth overseas members on their trip to Mt Egmont. Everything starts well: the sun is shining and we haven't been sitting on the seat at the coach stop very long before we're joined by two Australian brothers, Colin and Don who turn out to be fellows after my own heart. They have lived in New Plymouth for twenty months and will be returning home to Canberra at Christmas. Next July they're off to explore Britain and the Continent and after that plan to go on to Canada or South Africa. To my delight we sit with them in the back seat of the coach, together with a Dutchman, a New Zealander and an Englishman. Nothing gives me more pleasure than to be chatting with different nationalities and as we ascend Mt Egmont I'm in my element.

We stop at a hut near to the signposted Dawson Falls and are given the option of climbing down what we're warned is a steep and muddy path to view them. Dorothy says she's not interested, but even though I'm scared, I can't give up the opportunity of being with the lads who, anyway, are only too willing to give me a helping hand. It's well worth the effort for the sight of that tumultuous white jet of water rushing down from on high and plunging into a pool shot through with sunlight and surrounded by bush and trees is magical.

Back at base Dorothy, who can be so boisterous at times, has managed to fall into a swamp and hurt her leg. I feel irritated, even though there seems to be nothing unduly to worry about and I abandon myself to the sing-song in the hut before we return to New Plymouth. But back here, after we have a meal with the boys in a café and are making our way to The Chimes, Dorothy is in great pain with her leg and is limping badly.

I'm in a panic. How the hell are we going to get to the dance tonight with her like this? It became very obvious this afternoon that Don and I are madly attracted to each other and the thought of not seeing him tonight is unbearable.

Nothing for it though – we must find an emergency doctor. After examination and binding it, he says that he suspects a fracture and gives her a note for the hospital in Wellington. She hobbles back to The Chimes. Desperation drives me to suggest that we get a taxi to the dance, using as an excuse (albeit a perfectly legitimate one) that we must find out if we can travel back to Wellington on the coach with the others tomorrow.

"God knows what we'll do if we can't," I say. "We haven't enough money for the train and we certainly won't be able to hitch-hike."

I also point out that though she won't be able to dance, it would be very miserable staying in our room all evening. I feel guilty at pushing her so hard, but everyone fusses around her when we get to the dance, making sure she's sitting comfortably and bringing her soft drinks. Most importantly, we get the assurance that there will be space for us in the coach tomorrow.

My stomach continues to churn, nonetheless, for while all the fellows we met today are already here, Don is not. As if reading my thoughts, Colin bounds over and says that his brother will be coming later. In the meantime would I like to dance? All through the quickstep and waltz I cast surreptitious glances at the door, but it's not until we're sitting chatting that Don appears and immediately sweeps me onto the floor.

This turns out to be a fantastic evening. My delight is initially ruffled by guilt as we glide past the incapacitated Dorothy, but she soon she makes it known that she's tired and wants to go back to The Chimes. One of the overseas members offers to take her in his car. No, she says, when I ask her, she doesn't mind if I stay on for a while.

At 1 a.m. Don and I decide to go on to the all-night dance at the Taranaki Trades Hall. Here in the black-out waltz we exchange the first of many passionate kisses. Walking back to The Chimes later we chat as if we've known each other for years – about our families, our lives, our hopes for the future and agree how sad it is that with so much in common we have to part. We discuss, too, the chance of seeing each other again before he and Colin leave for Canberra in December. Perhaps I can come up to New Plymouth, I suggest; perhaps, he says, he can come to Wellington for a couple of days. He gives me his address in Canberra. He won't be there when I move on, he says, but he assures me his family would make me welcome. It's 4 a.m. before we can tear ourselves away from each other. As quiet as I try to be, Dorothy stirs.

"Only me," I whisper, "are you okay?"

"Mmmmmmmm."

My conscience pricks again. I really must be very nice to her tomorrow.

Monday 24 October 1955

I'm so tired I don't know what to do with myself. I sit on the coach in a trance, feeling detached from everything and everyone – well, that is, until I'm brought back to the real world when twelve miles out of New Plymouth, the front axle of the coach breaks. Inevitably this means a long wait to be rescued and we're led into a nearby paddock. True, it is a hot sunny day and we have a magnificent view of Mt Egmont, but this is the last thing I wanted.

Fortuitously, the secretary of the New Plymouth

overseas club has been following us in his car. He, therefore, races back to town for help and when he returns he comes bearing food and drink – bread and sausages, a keg of beer for the boys, cordial for us girls. Time passes, chatting, eating, singing and five hours later at 3.30 p.m. we're on our way. When we stop for tea at Wanganui Dorothy asks if I'd like to go hitch-hiking with her and some friends down the South Island at Christmas. It's a tempting offer, but I'm too exhausted to think about it at the moment. At 11.15 p.m. we arrive back in Wellington and I promise to give Dorothy a ring tomorrow evening.

Tuesday 25 October 1955

In the kitchen this morning Jean, one of our merry Hawker Street band, informs me that a man called me on Saturday. I guess it must have been Andrew off the ship. Then Grace tells me that she and Geurt saw Jorgen at the Empress Ballroom on Saturday and he asked after me. The irony is that after last weekend I don't give a damn about the Wellington men, my thoughts being wholly with Don in New Plymouth.

This afternoon Terry rings with a fantastic proposition. Back in her hometown of Southsea she belonged to an amateur dramatic group. One of its members, Peter, who became a close platonic friend, has recently come out to live in Auckland. He told Terry on the telephone that he's shortly buying a car and is planning a three-week camping tour of the North Island. Would she like to go with him and perhaps bring a friend? Whatever reservations I have about roughing it, this is an opportunity not to be missed and appeals to me much more than going off with Dorothy, so when I telephone tonight to find out how she is, I break the news. She doesn't seem particularly bothered, so that's all right.

Thursday 27 October 1955

I was right: it was Andrew, the ship's officer, who called at the weekend and I have arranged to go to the cinema with him tonight. But what an utterly bizarre evening this turns out to be. At 5 o'clock, as I approach Garland's, my mind preoccupied with how things will go later, I am surprised by a trilby-hatted figure stepping out from the doorway. It's John, the university student.

"Good evening Molly," he says lifting his hat and presenting me with a shoe-styled box tied with ribbon. "Please let me know your answer later."

Intrigued, I race up the stairs to the tiny room where we change into our overalls. Inside the box, arranged prettily on a bed of tissue paper are sprays of violets and a handwritten poem – all about the colour of my eyes and hair and how much he thinks about me and wants me to be his girlfriend. Would I consider it? I let out a roar and rush down to the kitchen to show Terry. We scream with laughter and Maria, who comes over to find out what all the commotion is about, shushes us.

"You know he's sitting out there in the restaurant," she whispers.

I clap a hand over my mouth, horrified, hardly daring to breathe while Maria peeks round the corner into the dining area.

"He's gone," she announces, "poor boy, you've frightened him off."

I feel absolutely dreadful. I may not be terribly interested in the guy, but I didn't mean to humiliate him. I have no option but to take the trophy on my date with Andrew.

"Been buying shoes?" he asks as I slip the box down by my feet in the cinema.

"Er – yes ......"

I like Andrew, but I'm a bit apprehensive when after the film he suggests a spot of supper on the ship. Although I don't refuse because the prospect of going aboard is exciting, I'm on edge. We eat supper in the mess area after which he suggests going to his cabin for a while. As soon as he takes off my blouse, I start to make excuses about being tired and having to get back to Hawker Street. He doesn't kick up a fuss or try to persuade me otherwise, but this, I know, is another one I won't ever see again.

Friday 28 October 1955

Terry rings. She's been talking to Peter about the forthcoming trip. The plan is for us to fly up to Auckland on Christmas Day. Oh boy – how exciting. This certainly gives an added gloss to the venture. Peter will meet us at the airport with the car. At the end of the holiday he proposes to drop us off at Taupo so we can hitch-hike back to Wellington.

Saturday 29 October 1955

At a ball at the New Settlers' Club tonight I'm partnered by one of the Dutch boys from Trentham, Benny. We're in the company of Benny's friend Hank and girlfriend Sylvia. I couldn't afford a new dress so Terry said I could borrow her satiny, gold-coloured one. Although I agreed, I don't like borrowing or, indeed, lending clothes. I used to let Jenny wear my jumpers sometimes at Trentham for fear of being considered a spoilsport, but it made me uneasy. This reluctance stems from Dad's attitude. When I was a baby, Mum told me, my Auntie Nell sent her a parcel of my cousin Joyce's cast-offs. Dad was furious and demanded they be sent back.

We have quite a jolly time this evening, lots of cigarettes and a couple of drinks and one or two dances, but I don't feel right in the dress and my hair, neck-length at the moment, is straggly and messy-looking. I am not helped either by the fact that Sylvia, who has naturally wavy hair, looks stunning in a strapless gown.

Wednesday 2 November 1955

This morning Jorgen the Dane rang and we arrange to go for a walk up Mt Victoria this evening. All he wants to do is to lie down and snog. His kisses are wet and sloppy and this puts me off completely. I shan't see him again.

Sunday 6 November 1955

I had thought John, the university student, wouldn't dare show his face again after the shoebox incident, but he turned up at Garland's again on Thursday and asked me to go for a drive with him this afternoon. This guy is a world apart from the males I've met since leaving England. It is ironic though – I would have given anything if one of his standing at the BBC had asked me to be his girlfriend. Why then does he irritate me so much? Why do I want to be outrageous and shock him? Perhaps it's the fact that he agrees with everything I say. Oh dear – I *know* I'm being horrid and bitchy, but I can't seem to help myself.

I ask him if I can have a go at the wheel of the car. The other Sunday when I went out with some of the New Settlers' crowd, this guy Bill let me drive the car for a short time and I managed very well. As reluctant as John is to concede to my request, he gives in and I'm doing nicely until we get to a road junction. At the moment the lights turn amber, I lose concentration and slam my foot down on the accelerator instead of on the brake. Cars screech to a halt and we end up practically on the kerb. I'm shaken and John doesn't hide his displeasure. I have a strong feeling I shan't see him again either, but really I don't care.

Friday 25 November 1955

It seems ages since John, Andrew and Jorgen were on the scene, not that I miss any of them, but I can't help feeling wistful when I see the rest of the gang getting on nicely with their beaux. As much as I'm enjoying the warmer weather (last Saturday Grace and I went down to Oriental Bay and sat on the beach) it makes me restless. Then, too, I get so melancholic and filled with yearning when I listen to the hit parade. My all-time favourite is *Unchained Melody*, which Terry and I play over and over again on the jukebox whenever we're in a milk bar. However, I'm far from being discontented with life generally. I still love my job at the Tourist Board and working at Garland's and rooming with Grace and I certainly wouldn't want to be back in Potters Bar. Also, of course, there's the keen anticipation of soon being on the road again, an event brought closer today when Terry and I purchase our tent.

Saturday 26 November 1955

I pop in and see Jenny this afternoon and as it's a brilliant day we decide to get the tram out to Worser Bay. This is on the opposite side of the harbour to Eastbourne and much further towards the Heads. Fantastic place – bushy backdrop to a shoreline strewn with rocks and boulders and beached sailing craft. I have a couple of dips in the ocean. Jenny and I talk endlessly about future travel plans, but I do wonder sometimes if they'll ever materialise.

Sunday 25 December 1955

This is an even stranger Christmas Day than last year at Trentham. After exchanging gifts with Grace, who is off to celebrate with Geurt at his sister's place, I make my way to Terry's. Here, before departing for the bus terminus, we eat a modest lunch of ham and lettuce, bread and butter and tinned fruit salad.

Everything feels so unreal, from walking in the warmth of the sun under a blue sky through a city devoid of humanity to being driven out beyond Paraparaumu to board our

National Airways Corporation plane. What a disappointment this is! I had this romantic vision of air hostesses gliding up and down spacious aisles, serving cocktails and whatever. The reality is a very small plane with only pocket handkerchief-sized windows and everyone wedged tightly into the seats. What's more, as the plane begins to dip and lurch, I feel sick, a feeling made worse by hovering for what appears to be an eternity above the airport at Whenoupai. Thank God we shall be hitching back to Wellington.

On terra firma again I quickly recover. My first impression of the tall, lanky and bespectacled Peter is of a rather serious, scout leader-type of young man. Almost at once he expresses concern at the size of our rucksacks because these have to be stowed on the back seat of the Renault where I have to sit as well.

"I didn't think you'd have so much," he says, "it's going to be a tight squeeze."

Before setting off we exchange Christmas presents – socks and hankies and soap. Tonight Peter tells us we'll be staying on a motor camp, but makes it quite clear that this is *not* a precedent.

"My idea is to get right away from civilisation and into the bush."

Oh Lord!

Tui Glen, just a little way out of the town, is spacious but filling up fast with trailers and trucks and American-styled cars. We select our spot and unpack. Peter says that after he's erected his tent, he'll show us what to do, but when that moment arrives, he looks puzzled on seeing our unfurled sheet of canvas.

"Where's the rest of it then?"

We stare at him blankly.

"The support pole and the pegs — surely you've got those?"

"This is all that the man in the shop sold us," Terry says.

Peter puts a despairing hand to his forehead. Terry and I can't help it; we start to laugh. Peter is annoyed. Curtly he tells us we'll have to improvise and orders us to go into the nearby bushes and find some stout sticks. Still chuckling over our folly, we do as commanded and then watch admiringly as our leader performs a miracle in staking our tent. But that's not the end of it. Standing back to survey his handiwork, Peter still seems to be troubled.

"It's much smaller than mine," he points out, "you're never both going to fit in there."

What we've done is inadvertently bought the single rather than the double size.

Peter sighs.

"Nothing else for it, you'll have to bed down in mine and I'll take yours."

Another serious boo-boo, but we dare not laugh this time. My spirits sink further when, in the course of setting up the primus stove and billycan, Peter says that although he'll cook tonight and in the morning, from then on we'll be taking it in turns. Hell's bells, I hadn't considered that aspect of the trip.

After tea, toast and boiled eggs, we go for a drive round Auckland. It's very humid tonight, not a breath of air and back at the ranch we're besieged by sand flies — the curse of our summer days at Trentham — and which now contribute to making this first night under canvas an absolute nightmare. The ground is incredibly hard and I toss and turn in my sleeping bag, hot, itchy and miserable, wondering if daylight is ever going to come.

*Peter's Renault in which he drove Terry and me 2000 miles round
the North Island on a 3-week camping tour,
December 1955/January 1956*

Monday 26 December 1955

Recovering from my night fears and physical discomfort once I've had breakfast and a thorough wash in the toilet facilities block, I'm filled with new bravado. What a performance though to decamp. I'm not the tidiest of people and Peter insists on everything being packed and folded up neatly so that it can be stowed away properly on the back seat of the car.

We head south to Rotorua, driving through the Waikato, an extensive farming area offering much the same scenic outlook as witnessed elsewhere in the North Island – rolling green hills, sheep, cattle, horses, sometimes orchards and nondescript towns like Hamilton and Cambridge. The best bit comes when Peter decides it would be interesting to make a diversion and have a look at the Atiamuri Hydro-Electric Power Station, one of many such sites being developed along parts of the Waikato River. This vast area of gouged earth and rubbled banks, of cranes and wire and workmen's huts, dramatically back-dropped by the conical wooded peak of Mt Powhataroa stirs my imagination. Although the technicalities of dam-building pass over my head, I marvel at the skill needed to create something on such a huge scale.

On we press towards Rotorua. In late afternoon, deep in countryside bereft of all other living creatures, the sky becomes ominously dark.

"That must be the town over there," Peter says, pointing to a roofed horizon.

There's a rumble of thunder.

"Do you think we can get there before this lot comes down and find a motor camp?"

Good old Terry, but Peter's having none of that and reiterates what he said last night about getting away from civilisation. Besides, he adds, he's the one who's been driving all day and he's tired. Soon on a slight ridge to the left of us we come across a ramshackle weatherboard house and decide to explore. Obviously it has long since been abandoned: grass grows high round its base, the paintwork is filthy, the windows splintered and holed and what remains of the glass is thick with grime. Peering in, we see a floor littered with broken beer bottles.

Adjacent to the house is a singularly tall tree standing at the head of a sloping field. This is where Peter decides we'll make camp. First though, because of the coming storm, Terry prepares supper and no sooner have we eaten and struggled to put up our tents in the rising wind, then the storm breaks. It could not be a fouler night: thunder and lightning crack the sky and we sit huddled in the Renault, watching the rain river down the windows. Peter lights a candle. Wanting to jot down what we've done so far, I fish in my rucksack for writing paper. Terry asks me what I'm doing. Immediately I feel self-conscious because no-one knows about my writing aspirations.

"Oh – just making a note of something," I say.

Inevitably the moment arrives when we must brace ourselves to run through the wet grass to our tents. Peter exhorts us not to touch the sides in case the whole thing collapses. Ye Gods! As we discovered last night, there's not room for us both to get ready for bed at the same time, so Terry shines a torch through the flap while I make up a pillow of towels, et cetera and gingerly ease into the sleeping bag.

If I thought last night was bad, this is a thousand times worse. The ground is as hard as ever, the wind howls and the tree next to the farmhouse never ceases to sigh and sough and creak. Suppose it uproots and crashes down on us? Suppose I accidentally touch the side of the tent in my sleep and we're buried under canvas?

Tuesday 27 December 1955

Daylight at last and the storm is over. Have I slept? I suppose I must have done, but it doesn't feel like it. Bleary-eyed, I mince over the wet grass towards the car.

"Your turn to cook breakfast," Peter greets me.

Dear God, not this on top of everything else. My throat tightens. I feel resentful.

"You'll have to show me how to get the primus going."

The result is disastrous. Confronted with a dish of congealed and half-burnt scrambled egg Terry and Peter gang up on me. Who can blame them? Their irritation is exacerbated further when we go in search of somewhere to wash the dishes. Everything is wet and misty and silent as we climb over a stile into a wooded area on the other side of the house. Eventually we come across a cattle trough, which Peter says will do fine. All goes well until, retracing our steps, I turn to look back and there on our heels are half-a-dozen cows. My stomach turns over.

"Oh my God!" I yell.

Peter tells me to stay calm and keep walking, but I can't resist turning round again. Petrified, I clutch at Terry's arm. She shakes me off scornfully.

"Oh don't be so silly – they're not going to harm you."

Nothing though can dispel the notion that any moment I'm going to be butted in the rear and I can't get over the stile quickly enough. Back at the car I feel contrite and to compensate for my stupidity make an extra effort to pack up efficiently. By the time we reach Rotorua harmony is restored and after a wash and brush up in a public convenience, I'm my old self again.

Sightseeing here, of course, is second-time round for me, but new for Terry and Peter. Nonetheless, I enjoy re-experiencing Whaka and the Buried Village, Tarawera and the Blue and Green Lakes. A real thrill this time is watching Maoris perform their ritualistic dances in the open – far more authentic and atmospheric than seeing it indoors. Once more I'm transported onto another planet by the rhythms and the vitality of the troupe. After the bad start to the day, things are turning out really well and my spirits only plummet again when Peter confirms that we shall return to last night's campsite. Ah well, at least it's not raining.

Wednesday 28 December 1955

Having slept quite well, I'm not nearly as lethargic and miserable as I was yesterday. Anyway, I'm looking forward to what surely will be one of the most exciting legs of our journey – driving round the East Cape from Whakatane to Gisborne.

I'm delighted that en route to Whakatane we stop off to take photos of the Wishing Tree (said to have been planted 400 years ago) along Hongi's Track. The site, chained off at the side of the road, has a plinth at each corner bearing a Maori figurehead. Along this track in 1823 Hongi Hika and his fellow Maori warriors, out on a warring expedition, carried their canoes from Lake Rotoiti to Lake Rotoehu.

Later we come in sight of the volcanic peak of Mt Edgecumbe, in the foreground of which rises the vast construction site of the Tasman Pulp and Paper Mill – a meccano-like complex of brick and steel, of cranes and towers and trucks. It excites me to think of great trees being felled and transported here.

Whakatane fires my imagination too. Its long Maori history is depicted by a model of an ancestral canoe, held aloft on trestle-styled supports at the base of a steep rocky escarpment. This is purported to have belonged to the Mataeutua tribe and transported here from Hawaiki about 1350 AD.

Now the really thrilling part of the journey begins. As we set off again under a sombre sky, no one on the road but us, I'm pumped up with anticipation. The scenery is wild and magnificent, the road turning and twisting through a green primeval world. When at last we come upon the sea in the late afternoon, it really does feel as if we've abandoned civilization. There's absolutely nowhere we could set up tents for the rough stony track runs between a grassy bank to the right and a wild, rocky beach on our left. Are we doomed to spend the night in the car? Strangely, I don't feel nearly as fearful as I did when we were in the heart of the countryside. The seascape is far more comforting. We carry on for a while. Peter is sure there must be habitation not far off, so he turns off the road and mounts the grassy bank. For ages we jolt along a muddy, rutted track, but at last a gate lies ahead of us.

"Right," he says, "I'm going to explore – you two stay here."

Twenty minutes pass. I start to get agitated, to create all sorts of horrific scenarios in my mind.

"I hope nothing's happened to him."

"Oh he'll be all right," says Terry.

Suddenly, out of seemingly nowhere, appear two or three cows and their calves. They surround the car and push their noses against the windows. Then one of the big ones puts his forepaws on the bonnet and we start to rock violently. I have visions of the car being upturned or rolling downwards. Terry and I shout and bang on the windows, but they are not to be budged and only vamoose when in the nick of time Peter returns and shoos them off.

He brings good news; there's a farm over the way, inhabited by a Maori family and permission has been given for us to camp on their land. It is comforting to know that there are other people around and as we come in sight of the house at the top of a gentle grassy incline, back-dropped by a clump of trees, the head of the household, a big smiling man, walks down to greet us.

"No need for yous to camp in the field," he says, "you can put your tents up on the lawn at the side of the house."

I could kiss the dear fellow, but Peter is not having any of that.

"We'll be absolutely fine down here," he insists.

How maddening he is at times and I curse inwardly as we pick our way over the cowpat-strewn grass. However, our Maori friend is not going to let us escape that easily. Soon he is back with an invitation: his wife insists that we join the family for supper. As reluctant as Peter is to take up the offer, he knows it would be churlish to refuse.

All my imaginings could not have come up with such an exhilarating and exciting evening and I have to keep telling myself that this is *not* a scene from a book or film. The discomforts and tribulations of this camping expedition so far are forgotten as we sit round a large wooden kitchen table, eating with this lovely, jolly family – Mum and Dad, their two handsome grown-up sons and delightful four-year-old daughter – and learning their history.

What a story they tell too. Dad was a bushranger in his youth; now he has an 80-strong herd of cattle. His wife's grandfather was a whaler, one of the first East Coast pioneers. She shows us a piece of embroidery she's doing – a wall-hanging for the new hall being built in the vicinity. One of the sons helps on the farm while the other works as a carpenter in Auckland. As for the little girl, she's been riding since she was two and goes to school on horseback every day. I could stay here all night listening to their stories and feel sad when it's time to leave them. Picking our way over the field by torchlight, I once again damn Peter for not letting us camp on the lawn.

Me before the isolated Maori farm on East Coast of the North Island, December 1955.

Thursday 29 December 1955

As usual I'm awake early and dying to go to the toilet. Cautiously I poke my head out of the tent to see cows grazing nearby, so I delay the ordeal for as long as I can. But soon our farmer friend arrives to say that his wife is preparing breakfast for us up at the house. The food is scrumptious – a feast of eggs and bacon and freshly baked scones. I come over sentimental and weepy as we say goodbye to these wonderful people, yet at the same time I'm invigorated and feel that I can endure any camping discomfort for the sake of this sort of experience.

The sea glitters in the sunlight as we start once more to judder and lurch over the rocky highway. From now on, whether we're in sight of the sea or driving inland, the scenery is magnificent. Near the coast we come upon a magnificent crimson-coloured Pohutakawa tree, while inland the high forest landscape abounds with bushes and trees of all shapes and sizes. Sometimes we come across a farm. Barefooted Maori children wave to us. On one occasion the road is blocked by sheep being herded by an old weather-beaten native, who wears a wide-brimmed hat and leads a packhorse.

At Waihau Bay we look across to Cape Runaway where the first whaling station in New Zealand was established, a reminder of our Maori friend's grandfather. Finally, rounding the promontory of the apex of the East Coast road we catch sight of what I consider the epitome of wild romantic scenery – surf rolling in over a wide expanse of deserted beach. This is Hick's Bay, named after Captain Cook's lieutenant.

It's sad that this part of the journey is over. Nothing to come can possibly match what we've seen and experienced in the last few hours. Nonetheless, I am delighted when, on the outskirts of what the signpost tells us is Tiki Tiki, Peter notices a roadside farm and decides to knock to see if we can camp on their land. Permission is given, but on this occasion the Maori family keep out of sight. Still, I feel safe here – that is until after supper when Peter suggests that we girls stroll over to the river to wash the dishes. To reach it we have to cross the road and enter a field, which is populated by a large and hefty-looking herd of cattle.

"D'you think," I venture to suggest, looking fearfully at two coal black, tail-swishing brutes, "that some of them could be bulls?"

"We'll be okay," says Terry.

Nothing, though, can diminish the churning of my stomach as we start to walk the length of the field. Soon there's a great thundering noise behind. I look round. The herd is charging our way. I urge Terry to run. No, she screams, we must *not* do that. If necessary, I'll take a running jump from the top of the bank into the river and risk a broken limb. This proves unnecessary. Something distracts the herd and they turn away.

"You see," says Terry scornfully, "they weren't chasing us after all."

I expect she's right as usual, but I can't relax until we're safely back with Peter.

Friday 30 December 1955

I come to with a start: an animal is sniffling and snuffling very close to me on the other side of the canvas. I tense, but force myself to sit up. A horse is poking his nose through the tent flap. It could be worse, I think and he soon wanders off.

I venture outside. No sun yet. There's not a soul in sight and the house looks dark and gloomy. I amble around till I find a sheltered grassy hollow to relieve myself, but then in full flow I suddenly become aware that I'm not alone and look up to see two little Maori girls staring at me. Not at all embarrassed, they smile and one of them thrusts out a wicker basket full of apricots.

"Yes, in a minute," I say, laughing and pulling up my pants.

After breakfast Peter says he wants to have a look at the church down the road before we go on our way. It is of some renown for it was built in 1924 as a memorial to a Maori soldier who died in World War I. We enter the grounds through a wide iron gateway, framed on each side by carved uprights, which support diagonal beams pinnacled with Maori carvings. In the church embroidered panels backdrop the altar, beneath which is a cross with the word 'Moku' written on it. I have the pleasing notion that given the remoteness of this area not many British people would have been in this church.

Peter is now anxious for us to replenish petrol and fast-dwindling food supplies. After what seems an eternity we at last come upon Ruatoria, home of the main East Coast tribe of Maoris and birthplace of politician Apirana Ngata in 1874. The sight of the main street filled with lorries and trucks, but flanked by wooden buildings with hitching posts for horses on the verandahs immediately conjures up in my mind childhood and Saturday morning cowboy films at the cinema.

We park and go into the corner shop. It's a good feeling to be stocking up on food, but fate is not kind to me. Forgetting to stash away the carton of eggs when we're putting our purchases into the back of the car, I accidentally sit on it. Given that we've been getting on each other's nerves the last couple of days, this incident provides the impetus for an explosion.

"Really Molly," Peter scolds, "You're so clumsy!"

Tears choke me. I apologise profusely and rush back into the shop to buy some more. To make amends I purchase a large slab of chocolate. But then, after having travelled a few more miles, I realise I've left it on the counter. This time there's no going back. Now it's Terry's turn to berate me. Cheeks burning, angry with myself and with her, I yell for Peter to stop the car.

"I know when I'm not wanted. I'll hitch back to Wellington *right now*.

"Don't be so stupid," Peter retorts.

An icy silence prevails and I sit in the back seat, battling with a lump in my throat and injured pride. Good humour is unexpectedly restored when we come across the mineral springs of Te Puia and discover that the mountain close by is called Mt Molly.

This is a haven of peace and beauty, the site consisting of nothing more than a rectangular-shaped swimming pool surrounded by trees and bushes. After all the frustrations of the morning, it's bliss to slip into the deliciously warm water and while away an hour, swimming and floating on our backs beneath a hot sun.

Refreshed, we carry on through a still wild and relatively deserted landscape, rough-forested hills vying with the coastal beauty of such bays as Tolago and Tokomaru. It's almost too much, sometimes, the scenery. If only it were possible to hold these images in mind permanently, but inevitably they all merge into one.

No wonder we are feeling weary at the end of this hectic day and I am so happy when Terry vocalises what I'm thinking – that a hot shower and decent toilet facilities would be very welcome. What a hope! Nonetheless, there is some compensation. We're not going to reach Gisborne by nightfall, so Peter decides we'll set up camp on a wild deserted beach – well, not on the sand itself, but on the grassy dunes leading down to it. The thought of breathing in salty air and being lulled to sleep by the roar of the surf is very appealing.

Saturday 31 December 1955

After the best sleep ever on this trip, I wake at 6 a.m. on this last day of 1955, bursting with energy. The other two, I know, will sleep for another couple of hours, so I dress and wander down to the water's edge. I walk the length of the beach, delighting in the early sunshine, the crashing surf and the solitude, squishing my toes in the wet sand and looking out to the horizon. What shall I be doing this time next year, I wonder, and most importantly, in which country?

After breakfast we proceed to Gisborne where we potter around and have lunch in a milk bar. Afterwards, strolling back to the car, a boy of about 11 years sidles up to Terry and me. If we go along with him, he murmurs, we can have *sex*. We're startled because this somehow doesn't fit in with the image of Gisborne as yet another run-of-the-mill suburban town.

We take a last look over the area from high on the coast road where a sign informs us that this is 'Young Nick's Head and Poverty Bay, 1605 ft above sea level.' Young Nick was Captain Cook's cabin boy and the first to catch sight of land at this point.

Mid-afternoon we reach a sign for Morere Hot Springs with the magical words 'Motor-Camp' written underneath. As it is impossible for us to reach Napier by tonight, Terry and I both urge that we stay here. Peter pulls a face, but this time we stand our ground, insisting that it is imperative we wash our hair.

"And it is New Year's Eve," I add, "it would be nice to have some company."

This is a secluded area encircled by tall waving palms. The campsite and facilities are adequate, but the evening is very warm and close and the sand flies are out in force. The suggestion that we have a dip after supper is therefore appealing.

The mineral baths are sited across the road from the camp and reached by walking along a bush track. Electric bulbs hung in the trees light our way. We swim in the mixed bathing pool, but the complex contains private baths as well, which are reached by other tracks. How eerie it feels and floating on my back, looking up at the trees and dark sky, I'm aware that this is a unique New Year's Eve experience.

Back on the campsite though, my expectations of communal Auld Lang Syne jollity soon evaporate in much the same way as they did in Auckland last year. All we get is a meagre explosion of fireworks and a few whistles blown, but everyone keeps to themselves. Shortly after midnight silence prevails.

Peter and I eating breakfast outside our tents at Morere Springs campsite, Sunday 1 January 1956

Sunday 1 January 1956

As always, I make New Year's resolutions, on this occasion determining that I *shall* carry out all my travel plans once the contract finishes in August. In such mood and with the sun shining, I embrace the idea of another swim in the pool before we head off to Napier.

Here again Terry and I are successful in persuading Peter to let us stay in the town's Kennedy Park Motor Camp which is splendidly modern and even has gas rings for cooking. After supper we drive along the front, once more familiar territory for me, but not for Terry and Peter.

Monday 2 January 1956

A welcome respite from packing up this morning for Peter decides we'll spend another night here. After breakfast we explore the Marine Parade and later drive out to Clifton Beach – but not to sunbathe or swim. This is near Cape Kidnappers, another spot named by Captain Cook following on the attempted kidnap by a Maori of his Tahitian servant boy who managed to escape and swim back to the ship.

Back in Napier there's a display of Scottish dancing in front of the arched shell-like edifice along the Marine Parade, also a bathing beauty contest. Peter is not all that interested and Terry and I make disparaging remarks about the girls. Afterwards we have supper in a milk bar, Terry and I heading straight for the jukebox.

Tuesday 3 January 1956

After the novelty and splendour of the East Cape, the ride south to Palmerston North through the now all too familiar pastoral landscape is very much an anti-climax. Unfailingly, as evening draws on, Peter starts up about camping in the bush. Fortuitously, as we near the town, the car starts to make funny noises. As this means leaving it in a garage overnight, we are forced to put up tents in the City Motor Camp.

Wednesday 4 January 1956

The car is running smoothly again as we head north-west, but the weather is not so good. Indeed, a storm is brewing as we approach Wanganui. I can't believe our luck when Peter drives us straight to the motor camp at the edge of the town on a bluff overlooking Castlecliff Beach. The facilities are basic, but there is a communal hut in which we spend an unexpectedly jolly and stimulating evening with three Danish lads, who are also staying here. How I adore European males, so different from English-speaking guys – as Grace and I discovered on our Austrian holiday.

Thursday 5 January 1956

The dawn world is chilly and dripping wet after a night-long downpour, but I am cheered by the Danish boys turning out after breakfast to wish us bon voyage as we set off for Mt Egmont. As it was in October when Dorothy and I were in the area, a weak sun appears as we start to snake up the mountain. Nonetheless, I'm far from happy when I realise that we have to sleep in a dark, dirty hut with iron-sprung bunk beds and a primitive smelly toilet.

Friday 6 January 1956

A ghastly night – I don't sleep a wink. The thought of spending another night here gives me the heebie-jeebies, but I dare not complain. This morning, Peter says, we're going to see how far we can climb up the mountain. It's a sunless, brooding sort of day as we get onto the path that ascends gently through bush and fern and tall trees. There is no-one around but us and this closeness to nature – the silence, the dank smell of vegetation and the shawl of mist drifting across the cone of Mt Egmont (said to resemble that of Mt Fujiyama in Japan) – gives me the creeps.

After a while Terry and I say we've had enough, but as Peter wants to go on, a compromise is reached: we'll return to the hut and see him there later. Time drags and we're bored, so we decide to walk a little way up the mountain again. Our thinking is that we shall probably bump into Peter coming down.

Reminiscing about the *Captain Cook* and Trentham as we amble along, disturbing the silence with bursts of raucous laughter, we lose track of time and place. Suddenly Terry looks at her watch and as there is no sign of Peter we decide to retrace our steps back to the hut. But now there's a problem – which of the two paths ahead do we take? We start with the one on the left, but it brings us back to our starting point, so we veer off to the right. The same thing happens again. I'm in a panic. Although scorning my idea that we're lost, Terry is also tense and tight-lipped. Once again we walk round in a circle, both of us getting more and more irritable. That's it, I decide, we're going to die up here on the mountain. Then – God knows how – we find ourselves on the right track for ahead of us is the opening out onto the flat which leads to the hut and, what's more,

Peter is striding angrily towards us.

"Where the hell did you two get to? I've been worried sick."

"We came to look for you," Terry says airily.

"You idiots! I've been back for ages."

"Just think," Terry jokes, "we could have been chasing each other up and down the mountain all day."

We shriek with laughter. This makes Peter more irate than ever. Don't we know, he says, that you *never* mess around on mountains? Poor old Peter!

Saturday 7 January 1956

Not even Terry and Peter have slept well, so we're all in a thoroughly disgruntled mood this morning. Today we're heading for Oeo, eighteen miles north of Hawera. Here Anne and John, a couple Peter met on the ship coming out to New Zealand, manage a farm. It's a stinking day, the rain heavy and persistent and the countryside looks grim as we trundle along in search of our destination. After a lot of dithering, Peter at last decides that the farm coming up on our left must be the one. All I can see through the rain-drenched widow is deep-rutted mud and a herd of dirty cows making for a barn. My spirits hit rock-bottom, but rise rapidly when we're warmly welcomed by Anne and John.

"Now," says Anne, after we have been seated in a warm, snug lounge and plied with tea and home-make scones, "you'll stay the night, of course. We've got two spare rooms and there are twin beds in one for the girls."

I can tell from Peter's face that he's going to resist.

"Oh, that'll put you to far too much trouble. We can sleep in our tents."

I hold my breath. *Please* Anne and John, I say to myself, *please don't listen to him.* They don't.

"That's ridiculous man," John says. "Do you really think we'd let you sleep outdoors in such terrible weather?"

What a nice couple they are, so quiet and unassuming and my delight is further compounded when after a delicious roast beef dinner they insist that we each have a bath. After all the discomfort of camping rough, can anything be better than to sink down into a tub of hot water, to come out feeling clean all over, then to slide between crisp white sheets, head cushioned on a soft pillow?

Sunday 8 January 1956

I can't believe it when I open my eyes and look at the clock – 10 a.m. Never before have I slept so late. To send us on our way Anne cooks sausages, eggs, bacon and tomatoes. Even Peter is in an extraordinarily cheery mood as we wave goodbye and set off for the Waitomo Caves.

Our route takes us northwards round Cape Egmont to New Plymouth and Waitara, travelling through yet another scenic landscape of rivers and hills and forest to Te Kuiti, a few miles south of the caves and our destination for the night. Here we are back to basic camping facilities, but I cheer myself up with the thought that it won't be too long now before we return to normal living.

Monday 9 January 1956

Exploring the Waitomo Caves – this millions-of-years-old

world of dark rivers and limestone formations, of stalagmites and stalactites which come in every shape and girth, some thin and needle-like, others chunky and ragged – is a feast for my imagination. In the Aranui Cave, founded in 1912, the stalagmites are as thick at their base as large trees and we see a variety of sculpted figures resembling well-known people. Our guide also points out the Crystal Palace and a 'hill' enclosing what is called 'The Garden of Allah.'

It is, however, the Waitomo Cave with its massive sculpted cathedral and organ that offers us the pièce de résistance. Proceeding down a long, damp stairway to the river, we come to a landing stage and step into a boat. A network of wires is strung around the walls and, apart from the sound of lapping water, we drift silently under a roof of green luminescence which emanates from the lava of hundreds of glow-worms. This is truly a magical sight. Afterwards at the kiosk I buy a set of snap-sized photos. These show the Queen and Duke of Edinburgh on their visit here in 1953.

This afternoon we head for Tongariro National Park. This brings back memories of last August and my miserable attempt at ski-ing. As we pass by The Chateau, I think how wonderful it would be to stay in there for the night. Instead, we end up pitching tents on the lower slopes of what I think Peter says is Mt Ngauruhoe. Whatever – while we have a splendid view of the countryside below, this is the most uncomfortable site yet, especially as there's a wind blowing. Not surprisingly, sleep evades me.

Tuesday 10 January 1956

I really am very tired of decamping and packing up the car. The trip has had many highlights but, by God, it's been an endurance test. I know Terry, too, has had enough. Only Peter remains indefatigable and as we make our way to Lake Taupo he is still making noises about camping in the bush. Once again Terry and I close ranks and we end up in the Municipal Motor Camp alongside the lake. Peter grumbles about the number of people around. One thing we all remark upon is how much we're the poor relations of the camping world. Near us, for example, is a large home-from-home tent with everything in it but the kitchen sink.

"They don't know the meaning of camping," Peter whispers scornfully.

Wednesday 11 January 1956

It is decided that we're not going to do anything special today, so we linger over breakfast then potter around Taupo, later going off in the car to the southern end of the lake to visit the small thermal reserve next to the government tourist hotel in Tokaanu. Here we have a leisurely swim in one of the mineral pools before returning to base. Over supper Peter tries to work out how many miles we've covered in the last three weeks and I muse on how strange it will be to get back to Wellington and work.

Thursday 12 January 1956

After visiting the Huka Falls – another first for Terry and Peter – we head for Wairakei, which like all other thermal sites has its own characteristics. Following the guide down a path beside the Wairakei stream in Geyser Valley, hung over with the usual sulphurous cloud of steam, the landscape is singularly surreal – silica terraces, bubbling mud pools and geysers bearing names according to what each resembles – the Dancing Rock, the Paddle Wheel and the Prince of Wales' Feathers.

Another rare and fascinating feature of the day is stopping off at the Karapiti Blow-Hole, reached from the road by a steep wooden-stepped and railed path. At the bottom, exploding with enormous force and at a temperature of 365°F is a jet of dry steam, which forcibly pushes out any object that may be thrown into the hole. Later we return to Taupo and have another swim in the mineral baths.

Friday 13 January 1956

As if we haven't experienced enough thermal activity, we spend our last sightseeing day at the Waiotapu Thermal Reserve, some miles north of Taupo. The magic of this site lies in its swathe of silica terraces and pools that reflect a variety of colours – pink, yellow, orange. The most fascinating of these is the Champagne Pool, diaphanous green water boiling at 197-212°F. Mud-pools, too, abound, chucking their evil-smelling slime high into the air. Lastly, there's the Knox Geyser. This is helped to perform at 10.15

each morning by the guide throwing in a handful of soap powder – what a cheat!

It's a fine warm evening for our farewell supper. We're chummy and relaxed and in reminiscent mood. Even my gaffes, the cause of so much irritation, are remembered with amusement and I have to admit that, despite everything, it has been a great experience and one I wouldn't have missed.

Saturday 14 January 2006

Peter says he'll wait by the roadside until we get a lift.

"Making sure you get shot of us once and for all, eh?" Terry jokes.

"Of course!"

More good-humoured banter before we're dwarfed by a huge army lorry coming to a halt beside us. The window is lowered.

"We can take you as far as the Desert Road," the driver says.

Peter, I'm sure, will never forget the last sight of us, bums stuck up in the air as with a great deal of huffing and puffing and help from the soldiers we laughingly heave ourselves into the driver's cabin. As we get going they explain that because military personnel are not supposed to carry civilians they'll have to drop us off long before we reach the army camp at Wairou. Just as well seeing how cramped we are – me squeezed between the driver and his mate, Terry sitting on the latter's knee. Still, we have great fun flirting with them.

Our good fortune continues with three more easy pick-ups in family cars, but by the time we reach Palmerston North, we're exhausted and the thought of hitching the last

90 miles to Wellington is just too much to contemplate.

"What about taking the train from here?" I suggest.

"If we've got enough between us for the fare," Terry says.

We sit on a station bench and count our money and, yes, we can just about do it. The bugbear is that we have to wait over an hour for the Wellington train. As for the journey itself, shall we ever get there, we keep asking? The only thing that sustains us is the thought of hot food, hot bath and soft bed.

Monday 30 January 1956

Is it only two weeks since we returned to normal life after our epic three weeks away? In England I always felt so discontented on returning from holiday, but it is not the same here. I never tire of the day-to-day routines of Wellington life – busy hours in the office, hammering at the typewriter and the not-so-busy ones when there's time to chat with the girls, flirt with the men and go to the milk bar for morning coffee with Tom. Then there's the 5 o'clock rush to get to Garland's, the pleasure taken in remembering half-a-dozen orders simultaneously, in being complimented on efficient service, on setting up tables for the next day, Theo making jokes, Maria clucking like a mother hen. The only times I feel uneasy are when the old man is on the prowl and in a bad mood – not that he says much to us girls, but he does go on at Maria.

Regularly, too, I go back to Terry's place after we've finished at Garland's. Here we drink black coffee and eat chocolate biscuits, listen to the Hit Parade and endlessly discuss travel plans for when our contract finishes. These change all the time. One minute I'm thinking I wouldn't mind going south for a while to Mt Cook and Milford Sound, perhaps work as a waitress in hotels, then I read something in the office about Norfolk Island and Terry says what about Fiji? Ah now – *Fiji* – the thought of living and working on a tropical island in the Pacific sounds very exciting.

"Why don't we write to the High Commission?" I suggest.

Sometimes we go to the cinema. As Shirley is no longer with us at Garland's I also enjoy going to see her in Kelburn for a good gossip. I'm very fond of her, she's so easy to get on with and never bitchy. Even Saturday household chores in Hawker Street are relieved by chats with Grace, or messing around with the rest of the crazy gang. Sometimes Grace and I go down to Oriental Bay, or I may pop up to Jenny's place where she always seems to be holding court with the Dutch boys.

Saturday evenings are the only times I feel lonely, especially when the lights are dimmed for the Last Waltz at the Empress Ballroom. Not even bopping to Bill Haley's *Rock Around the Clock* with Frances, Ella and Lois can eliminate the fact that I have no boyfriend at present.

Friday 3 February 1956

I can't believe my luck when this good-looking blonde guy, Trevor, pays me almost undivided attention at the New Settlers' Club social. He has a car and drives me back to Hawker Street. One kiss and I'm on fire. We get into the back seat. Never have I felt such intense desire, yet I know I can't let myself go and to give him his due he doesn't try and persuade me otherwise. I had hoped though that he might suggest going on to the all-night dance at the Empress, but no such luck. However, I'm far too churned up to go to bed and make a snap decision. Damn it, I'll go to the dance on my own. This turns out to be an unwise move for there on the floor is Trevor wrapped around a blonde who from the look of her will no doubt give him what he wants later. I return to Hawker Street, sick with envy and frustration.

Sunday 19 February 1956

With Mick away at sea again for a long spell Terry suggested a couple of weeks ago that we join the All Nations Club. On our first visit she gets friendly with these two rather posh older guys – Arthur (an accountant) and Eddie (a tailor). They are pleasant enough in a non-sexual way. This afternoon Arthur takes us for a drive to Raumati in his smart car.

Thursday 8 March 1956

Yippee – a letter from Anne and Noel in Christchurch inviting me for Easter again. They've now moved to a suburb called Spreydon, ten minutes away from the city centre.

Thursday 29 March 1956

We're hellishly busy at Garland's and Maria isn't too pleased that I have to dash off to the docks to get the ferry to Lyttelton. I'm hot and flustered as I go up the gangplank, but soon relax as I get caught up in the hustle and bustle of finding my cabin. On this occasion I'm sharing it with Margaret, a pleasant New Zealand widow, who's just spent six months in the States with her married daughter. Back up on deck to watch departure, two stewards begin chatting to me.

"You say you came out on the *Captain Cook*? She's in port at the moment – look over there."

All I can think of is that soon I'll be sailing away in a much larger vessel to another country. At this point a young male passenger, Kevin, joins us. He lives in Christchurch, but hails originally from Dunedin. We talk non-stop and go into supper together – bread and butter, cheese and biscuits and tea. When I return to the cabin Margaret is asleep.

Good Friday 30 March 1956

The train arrives at Christchurch at 7.30 a.m. Anne is not on the platform, so I have a cup of tea and sandwich in the station buffet and it is there that she finds me. She overslept, she says, and Noel is still in bed.

The new flat, which they rent unfurnished for £3 per week, is actually half a house, the other part occupied by the landlady and her husband. Once more I have to admire their practical skills. Noel made the settee and chairs, Anne the bright red cushions.

It's bitterly cold this Good Friday, so we sit all day in front of a roaring coal fire, catching up on news and eating. I sleep on a borrowed camp bed, which is much more comfortable than my lumpy old mattress in Hawker Street.

Easter Saturday 31 March 1956

What luxury – Anne brings me breakfast in bed. Today the weather is warmer and by the afternoon the sun is hot enough to sit out on the front porch. About 3 o'clock friends arrive, Eileen and Ron and their son Paul. I learn from the conversation that we're all going to a party tomorrow night at the house of other mutual friends, Pam and Jack who have two children and one on the way. Jack, Anne tells me, is a cinema manager in Christchurch. Pam works in the office of a department store, but also advertises clothes on the radio. They seem to be such fun people, so different from their counterparts in Potters Bar. Where did they meet them all, I want to know?

"On the ship coming out," Anne says, "if it weren't for them, we wouldn't have any friends."

This makes me realise that while I get on very well with the New Zealanders at work and elsewhere, my close pals are all English. I ask Anne and Noel if they intend returning to England in the future. Basically, yes, in about three years' time, but they're ambivalent about it, for they also would like to buy a house and start a family and Anne admits that the urgency to go back just isn't there any more. She finds this frightening. I tell them that when I return to England eventually, I wouldn't be able to live in Potters Bar again. Anne understands only too well. She says that she felt the same way about Cumberland after returning from Australia and that's why she ended up in London and at the BBC. The best thing for me, she thinks, is to live in a hostel for a while in order to make new friends.

This evening Noel has booked tickets for the cinema.

Performances are not continuous as they are at home, so you can't turn up in the middle of a film, or if you wish – as we sometimes did – sit through the whole programme again.

Easter Sunday 1 April 1956

The spoiling goes on with breakfast in bed yet again. This is followed by a lazy morning and another delicious roast dinner.

We're the last ones to arrive at the party, but what a welcome we get. In an atmosphere buzzing with chatter and Glenn Miller music, Jack thrusts a glass of Pimms into my hand and Pam introduces me to everyone. All the married couples are English, as is Bill, the single guy from Yorkshire, but there are two New Zealand girls, one of whom works with Pam. I'm in my element, talking, smoking, drinking and playing games. In the one called *Judge and Jury*, I'm 'convicted' of leading Bill astray and as 'punishment' have to dance the hula-hula with him. Now on my third Pimms I have no inhibitions and lap up the acclaim I receive. Suddenly my head starts to go round and round and, horror of horrors, I feel sick. I stop abruptly, face draining of colour.

"Are you all right?"

"No, feeling a bit woozy – I think I must have a cold coming," I reply, desperate not to disgrace myself.

The truth is that the alcohol has gone straight to my head. I remember going out with Terry and some of the lads at Trentham to a hotel in Lower Hutt one Saturday afternoon. I felt exactly the same as I do now and, indeed, back at the hostel was violently sick. At least here I'm not physically sick but I can't carry on and take up Pam's suggestion that I lie down in the spare room. As I still feel rough a couple of hours later, it's decided that I should stay the night and go back to Spreydon in the morning.

Easter Monday 2 April 1956

The kids running through the house wake me. I remember where I am and what happened and when Pam appears with a cup of tea, I apologise profusely. She's really very nice about everything and says she's just glad to know I feel all right. After breakfast Jack drives me to the square where I get the bus to Spreydon. Anne and Noel have been concerned about me and decide I must have caught a chill. I don't disillusion them. After a stroll through the city, we have an early dinner before the taxi arrives to take me to the ferry.

Last year when I left Christchurch it seemed probable that I would see Anne and Noel again, but this time – who knows? A few nostalgic moments, but these are soon dispelled on boarding the ferry. As I lean over the rail to watch departure, two young Kiwi fellows approach me and invite me to have a drink with them at the bar. We're there joined by no less than eight members of the Wellington Football Club. One of them takes my telephone number because, he says, the club needs girls for parties and dances in the winter months. Here's hoping…..

Thursday 12 April 1956

Oh dear, what's happening to everyone? Work colleague, Gillian, got engaged at Easter. Already she's talking excitedly of buying a section and building a house – God, how boring! Much more thrilling is the news that Jenny's Frits is off to see his father in America next month and the plan is that Jenny will join him later in the year, after she's been back home to see her folks. Grace is also planning to go home about October and see her family before returning to marry Geurt. So – with Shirley still going strong with Sepp and Terry with Mick, I feel very much out of it.

Wednesday 18 April 1956

I decide this week that depressing as it is going to be without a boyfriend on the occasion of my 21st birthday on 18 May, I must celebrate somehow. After discussing it with Grace and the others, I plump for a dinner at the Royal Oak Hotel on Saturday, the 19th. There'll be ten of us. In Mick's absence, Arthur and Eddie, our All Nations Club friends, say they are happy to escort Terry and me and as Frits will have departed for the States, one of the Dutch boys will accompany Jenny. Then, of course, there'll be Grace and Geurt and Shirley and Sepp.

Friday 20 April 1956

At lunchtime Terry comes along with me to the Royal Oak to discuss menus. I opt for starters of either fruit cocktail or crème of mushroom soup, followed by baked fillet of sole, roast stuffed duckling, desserts and coffee. It doesn't seem right to be ordering my own birthday cake, but there's no-one else to do it. I decide to have it made entirely of ice cream with 'Happy 21' scrolled on it.

Saturday 5 May 1956

Jenny and I take a trip to Eastbourne after lunch. She said farewell to Frits this week and is feeling sad, but oh what an exciting future she has ahead of her and on this gloriously sunny autumn day my urge to emulate her becomes even more pressing. We have a super afternoon, walking the boulder-strewn beach and clambering over rocks. Looking out to the sea glittering beyond the Heads, I am filled with expectations of a glorious future.

Friday 18 May 1956

When I think of my cousin's 21st birthday party in 1950 and the agonies I suffered because of Dad's unsociability, I'm so glad I'm not celebrating mine at home. Yet, I feel guilty at not sharing this day with my parents and decide to cable flowers with a message thanking them for letting me come to New Zealand.

What a fuss they make of me in the office. I'm particularly thrilled with a card, hand-drawn and painted by the Art Studio: here we all are in caricature, me in tight skirt and high heels, disappearing round a corner, peered after by male colleagues. At lunchtime I buy cakes for everyone and at tea break in the canteen I'm presented with a Rhinestone necklace and earrings and a large bunch of flowers. Yet again, I think how lucky I am to work with such a lovely crowd.

Saturday 19 May 1956

I spend ages getting ready tonight and am very pleased with the result. My hair, always so temperamental, goes well and in my new black grosgrain dress, set off by the Rhinestones, I feel very sophisticated.

At the Royal Oak I sit at the head of the table with Arthur opposite. The girls give me some lovely presents – a scarf, perfume, a marcasite ring and more earrings. We are all in a jolly mood and the food is good, the ice cream cake perfect and the waiter obliges me by taking a couple of photos. It's still early when we finish so Arthur and Eddie suggest we go back to their place for a bit of a party. This is an unexpected kindness, but as the evening draws to a close, I feel sad, namely because there's no-one special to make a fuss of me.

My 21st birthday celebration at the Royal Oak Hotel, Wellington on Saturday 19 May 1956 – l. to r. Grace, Jenny, Me, Terry, Shirley

Thursday 24 May 1956

Ashore again, Mick asks Terry to marry him. Although I expected this, it brings me to earth with a bang and I have to do some hard thinking. Do I really want to go down to the South Island or hop over to Fiji or Australia *on my own*? Suppose...... I just go back to England? Of course, it seems a shame not to have seen these places, but on the other side of the world the whole of Europe waits to be explored. What's more, there would be another five weeks at sea to look forward to, this time as a fare-paying passenger *and* travelling via the Suez Canal, the route which has lots of exotic stopping-off places to visit. The more I think about it, the more excited I get and already imagine myself arriving at Tilbury or Southampton, looking very glamorous in a new suit and high heels and – I fancy – a large picture hat. Yes, this is what I shall do!

Monday 28 May 1956

Terry rings me. She's discovered that girls are wanted to serve cups of tea and clear tables at what are commonly known here as 'The Trots' (horse-drawn carriage races) and there's a fixture at the Parkway Racecourse in Lower Hutt on Saturday. We can get there and back by bus from the station. I'm all for it – anything to boost the savings.

Saturday 2 June 1956

It's an early start this morning. The facilities at Parkway are basic and because we're not on the go the whole time, we manage to see snatches of the races. What amazes me is the speed at which these small horse-drawn carts can travel. On returning to Wellington I feel great satisfaction about having more money to put into the post office account on Monday.

I haven't made any arrangements to go out tonight and back at Hawker Street, where Geurt has recently arrived, my spirits droop.

"Why don't you come to the Empress with us Molly?" Grace asks.

"Oh I can't do that – I'd be playing gooseberry."

"No you won't. Heavens, Geurt and I are well past that stage now. Do come."

Well, I suppose it's better than sticking around here, feeling sorry for myself, even if I do end up as a wallflower.

As always the fellows are clustered just inside the door. I try to look unconcerned, but soon after Geurt has led Grace onto the floor, this dark-haired guy, impeccably dressed in dark trousers, white shirt, collar, tie and smart blazer, asks me to dance. Ken is from Glasgow and he's been in New Zealand for only two months. He has a bedsit not far from Hawker Street, but is working as an engineer on a cargo ship plying up and down the coast. Anyone with a Scottish accent and to do with ships must attract my attention, but that aside, he seems really nice and I wonder if he'll ask me to dance again. In the meantime two more guys get me up on the floor and when the Last Waltz is announced Ken approaches and afterwards suggests that we go for coffee in town.

In the milk bar he tells me about himself. His father was a miner, but following his mother's death when he was 6 years old, he and his two brothers, John and Norman, were shunted around from mining family to mining family because his father couldn't cope with looking after them. When his Dad eventually re-married and had a daughter, they all lived together again. However, the boys hated their stepmother and one by one left home to join the forces. Ken joined the RAF (hence the badge on his blazer) and served eight years, the last three of which he was stationed in Germany.

Earlier this year his Dad, who had brought his second family to New Zealand, suggested that Ken join them in Lyttelton to help run the milk bar he had set up there. But they didn't get on, his Dad threw him out and he came up to Wellington. As for his brothers, they too left the forces; John went to sea and Norman is thinking of coming out to New Zealand. There is also family in Wellington: elderly Aunt Ellen, who as a young woman emigrated to Wellington, her son Athol (Ken's cousin) and wife Lorna, but he has not yet contacted them.

He kisses me goodnight on the doorstep of No. 4 and tells me he's away up the coast for a while, but perhaps he'll see me at the Empress again sometime. I wonder......

Friday 15 June 1956

Grace is very pleased. She's got herself a part-time job at Thwaites, a catering company which employs, she was told, "only very nice girls" to serve drinks at parties, weddings and balls. Sounds super and the pay is good too.

Friday 22 June 1956

Great excitement in the office this morning – four members of the South African rugby team, the Springboks, who are here to play against New Zealand's All Blacks, come into the office to see our Assistant Director, Mr. Williams. They are accompanied by their manager, Dr Craven and the South African press people. I'm flattered when Mr. Williams tells me later that one of the players was creeping up behind me down the corridor and studying the names on the door when I went into my office.

At lunchtime I meet Terry and we go into the DIC to find my 'going-home' suit. It is a dream – ice-blue, trimmed with black around the neck and pockets, a straight skirt and jacket nipped in at the waist, with three-quarter length sleeves. I put it on lay-by: this means paying £1 per week off it for the next twelve weeks. Yesterday, too, Grace found a dressmaker who doesn't charge the earth, so I'm going to start looking for some material to have things made up for the ship. Getting ready for another long voyage across the world fills me with joy and I'm in such good humour that after Garland's, I pop into the Servicemen's Shop to look for gifts to take home. To my delight some of the Springboks are here too, looking at paua shell brooches, powder compacts, etc.

Saturday 23 June 1956

Grace is working at Thwaites all day and Jenny pops down this afternoon. I tell her about the rugby match. We listen to it on the wireless and because the Kiwis are so smug about their sporting achievements, we're delighted that the Springboks win.

As soon as Jenny goes home, Grace arrives back with a small joint of beef. We have this with baked and boiled potatoes, peas and carrots. Afterwards, while she is getting ready to go to the Empress with Geurt, she again persuades me to go with them. Fate indeed for Ken is there with two other guys who came over on the ship with him. This time we dance together a lot and later over coffee he asks if I'd like to go for a walk tomorrow afternoon. I suggest that he comes back to Hawker Street afterwards for tea.

Sunday 24 June 1956

Rarely does the Hawker Street gang – Grace and me, Dot and Val, Rita and Jonesie – descend upon the kitchen at the same time to cook Sunday dinner, but today here we all are and in very high spirits.

"What's in here?" I ask Dot, peering into her saucepan boiling away on the stove, "looks like dirty socks to me."

She pokes me in the ribs and feigns indignation.

"I'd have you know Molly Baxter, these are lamb chops."

"Ugh!"

The laugh, however, is soon to be on Grace and me. Dessert is to be a small plum pudding. For lack of a basin we plunge it into a pan of cold water and leave to boil on a high gas while we have the rest of the beef. Alas, on returning to the kitchen, we find that the pan has boiled dry and the greaseproof paper burnt to a cinder. Grace, however, is determined we shall eat it.

"I'll make some custard," she says.

"But we haven't got a clean saucepan."

"We'll use the one we did the peas in. It all goes down the same way."

So, it is burnt pudding, topped with pea-flavoured custard, not our best culinary effort.

Grace then goes off to spend the rest of the day with Geurt and his sister and I pretty myself up for Ken. He arrives at 2.30, looking very smart in his RAF blazer and bearing camera and a pile of records – Dean Martin, Nat King Cole, Mario Lanza. I think he would like to stay in, but I couldn't possibly do so on such a glorious day.

We head up to Mt Victoria. I never tire of the view of Wellington from here, fold upon fold of encircling hills, cascades of houses, then the harbour itself with all sorts of vessels at anchor and a cargo boat beginning its voyage to God knows where. From here we carry on to Hataitai, through attractive residential areas where some of the wooden houses are painted pastel colours. Then, finding a way down to the coast road, we return to Hawker Street via Balaena and Oriental Bay, past the boat harbour, everything tranquil but brilliant, the sea deep blue.

I had planned on egg and chips for tea, but there are not enough potatoes so it's boiled eggs and toast, with tinned pineapple to finish off. Afterwards we listen to Ken's records and he goes at 10 p.m. Wednesday he's taking me to the cinema.

Tuesday 26 June 1956

I receive my usual weekly letter from Dad. Things are

looking up in Potters Bar – Mum has had a *blue rinse* in her hair. Interestingly, Dad mentions an article in *The People* about this girl emigrating to New Zealand "in search of a bronzed sheep farmer." Well, good luck to her. From what I've seen and experienced it's all drink and sport with Kiwi men, girlfriends and wives coming a poor third. At parties I've noticed how the women always congregate together while the men distance themselves and see how much beer they can guzzle in the shortest possible time. What really infuriates me is their God's-own-country complex and bad sportsmanship – for example, the excuses I had to listen to in the office the last two days as to why they lost the rugby last Saturday.

Wednesday 27 June 1956

I'm horrified when Ken turns up for the cinema wearing one of those ghastly flat working men's caps. Dear God, I hope I don't see anyone I know. So strongly do I feel about this that when we come out of the cinema and he goes to put it on again, I have to say something. I don't want to hurt his feelings, so I try to be diplomatic by saying that I have an aversion to men in hats and, anyway, he looks so much nicer without one. He's surprised, but stuffs it back in his pocket.

Over coffee, he reminisces about his three years in Germany with the RAF – the happiest time of his life so far. This leads onto the subject of his Dad once again.

"Guess what? He's now demanding I repay the money he forked out for my passage to New Zealand. If I had known he was going to treat me like this, I would never have left the RAF."

With hindsight, perhaps, I shouldn't have questioned him further, but he's so bitter and I'm curious. When I learn that as a small child he witnessed his father throwing a carving knife at his mother (fortunately it missed and hit the kitchen wall), I'm filled with such horror that my stomach turns right over. I can't imagine *anyone* doing something as dastardly as that.

Saturday 30 June 1956

Tonight Ken and I meet up with Terry and Mick for drinks at the Royal Oak. We all get on well and pass a pleasant evening together. Ken's off up the coast again on Monday. Strangely that doesn't bother me too much. Although it's great to have a boyfriend again, this doesn't mean I want him round me all the time. Indeed, I can't really fathom out my feelings for Ken. The workman's cap and family history I find very disturbing and unsettling, but isn't that just being snobbish? Also, although I feel quite comfortable with him, he does very little for me physically, especially when I think how past boyfriends have aroused me.

Wednesday 4 July 1956

I have begun to take an interest in matters that once would have bored me silly, for example, the South East Asia Treaty Organisation (SEATO). This has come about because at work I have to type out confidential reports and articles for Mr. Bryant, who handles publicity for the government's External Affairs Department. Books, of course, have always played a major part in my life, but non-fiction reading has hitherto concentrated mostly on the lives of eminent literary figures of the past. Now I've widened that and have just finished reading *Venture into Darkness*, an absorbing book about the rescue of an American businessman from communist China. Terry's a great reader, too, and we often spend lunch-hours in the library.

One thing I feel guilty about is how much I've neglected my own writing since coming here, but lack of privacy and not having a typewriter of my own makes it difficult. I resolve to get down to it in earnest when I'm back in England.

Thursday 12 July 1956

11 p.m. and Grace and I have not been long in bed when Rita knocks at the door.

"Molly – telephone for you."

It's Ken, not long back from the sea. He wants me to meet him in town for coffee because he's something to ask me. I'm intrigued and excited at the idea of going out on a date at this time of night. As I rip off my pyjamas and put on fresh make-up, Grace looks at me as if I've gone crazy. From the moment I sit down opposite Ken in the milk bar, he's very attentive, even holding my hand across the table. He says he's done a lot of thinking on this last voyage and has realised he's in love with me. Would I marry him? I'm both flattered and panicky and tell him he's taken me by surprise and suggest we talk about it again on Saturday.

My brain teems as I slip into bed and sleep is impossible.

Is Ken really Mr. Right? Do I love him? If so, why doesn't he arouse me sexually? Perhaps that will come later. But what about the cloth cap and his awful father? And then, oh God, the most important thing – what about all my travel plans and going back to England? On the other hand, how wonderful to be in the swing of things like the other girls, to have someone special in my life, to lose my virginity at last… also…. suppose we get married, but don't *settle down*…….?

Saturday 14 July 1956

In the coffee bar after the cinema, I tell Ken exactly how I feel about the future – that although I've had a super time in New Zealand and am not averse to getting married, I don't want to settle down here and be lumbered with house and mortgage.

"To be absolutely honest with you Ken, although I've told Mum and Dad I'm going home at the end of the year, what I would really love to do is to live in Australia for a while, *then* return home."

Well, he says, there's nothing to keep him in New Zealand either, but the problem is he hasn't got the money to travel at the moment. *Is that all?* I point out that I have enough saved to take us both to Australia and he's *not* to protest, because if we are married, what's mine is his and vice versa.

"Think of the fun we could have," I enthuse, "and just as long as we return to England after a couple of years, I'm sure my parents will understand."

We talk and talk and talk. He says he'll give up the ship and get a job ashore – preferably in an office, I suggest. He agrees and great waves of excitement surge through me. How fantastic to meet someone who thinks like I do – what a triumph! See, I want to shout to the world, marriage can be exciting and different.

Sunday 15 July 1956

Grace and Geurt are taken aback at the news.

"He's a nice guy," says Geurt, "but Molly this is very quick. You've only known him a few weeks."

This reaction unsettles me and in view of the Laurie fiasco last year, I decide to say nothing in the office yet, nor to Maria and Theo at Garland's.

Monday 16 July 1956

I'm itching to type a letter to Mum and Dad, but I'm busy this morning and my only opportunity is when Gillian goes off to lunch. I can't help gloating over the fact that this is not going to be a conventional marriage and while I know they're going to be very disappointed not to see me at the end of the year, I stress that Ken has promised faithfully that we'll return to England in two years' time.

While we're changing into our overalls at Garland's, I tell Terry the news. Her reaction is not what I expect.

"I don't think he's the right one for you Molly."

My hackles rise and I remind her that she said she liked him when we all met up.

"But you hardly know him."

Oh God! Why does everyone have to be so stuffy?

Thursday 19 July 1956

I've had a super idea. The New Settlers' Ball is on Friday 10
August. By that time Ken will have given up his sea job, so
why don't we get engaged then? He agrees. After Garland's
I go up to Kelburn to tell Shirley: she doesn't say much, but
I think she's pleased for me.

Friday 20 July 1956

Ken rings to say he's spoken on the telephone to cousin
Athol and wife Lorna, the outcome of which is we have an
invitation to go to dinner with them in Wadestown on
Sunday. He mentions that his Aunt Ellen, who had a mental
breakdown a few years ago, is going to be there as well. Oh
well, I suppose this is a visit we have to make, but I suggest
we don't say anything about our forthcoming engagement
on this occasion.

Sunday 22 July 1956

As soon as we arrive in Wadestown at about 12.30 and are
ushered into an immaculate house, I know why I wasn't
looking forward to today. New Zealand suburbia is as
deadly as Potters Bar. My spirits plummet even further
when introductions are made. Aunt Ellen is a typical old
lady, big and bosomy and not much to say for herself. Athol
is pleasant enough in a nondescript fashion, but Lorna is the
sort of practical woman (short mannish hair, floppy slacks)
with whom I find it difficult to empathise. At her suggestion

Athol shows us round the house and garden while she and Ellen see to dinner. I feign interest, but really I'm bored to tears and leave it to Ken to make comment. Still, I have to admit that Lorna can cook – the roast chicken and apple pie are superb and I perk up at the mention of going for a drive round Days Bay when the washing up is done.

My euphoria does not last long. Lorna and Athol spend the whole journey pointing out properties and prattling on about the cost of buying a section. I sink into apathy. By the time we get back to Wadestown, I'm in sulky, rebellious mood and when Ken insists on taking a photo of us all standing by the car I refuse to smile or even to look at the camera. The only thing that cheers me is our departure after tea.

"You must come again soon," Lorna and Athol insist.

Not if I can help it, I think, and thank God that we won't be staying in Wellington after the wedding.

Thursday 26 July 1956

All week I've been thinking about the dress I shall buy for my engagement on 10 August and today at lunchtime I make my choice – a gorgeous mid-calf, full-skirted blue chiffon over taffeta with halter neck.

Wednesday 1 August 1956

Dad's long-awaited letter arrives with favourable response to my news. Yes, of course, they're disappointed I shan't be returning home this year, but the most important thing for them, Dad writes, is my future happiness. He also says that

Ken sounds a very nice man and he and Mum look forward to meeting him eventually. Dad has come up trumps again.

Thursday 2 August 1956

My subtle encouragement to steer Ken towards a white-collar job has sunk in. Now permanently on land, he rings to say that next week he has an interview with the Post Office for the position of clerical officer.

Friday 3 August 1956

After Garland's tonight Ken and I shop for an engagement ring. I know he can't afford very much, but I'm more than happy to have the smallest, cheapest diamond we can find. I point out that it's much more important to put the money we're saving towards our travels rather than spend it all on this white wedding nonsense. The suit, which was to have been my going home outfit and which I'm still paying off, will be ideal for a Registry Office ceremony.

Friday 10 August 1956

Ken rings to say he's got the job in the Post Office. The news gives me a terrific boost and I get ready for the New Settlers' Ball feeling happy and confident about the future. Ken tells me I look lovely and I'm proud of him too. The evening goes very smoothly. We dance a lot, have a photo taken and chat endlessly about our plans.

Monday 13 August 1956

There's only one doubting Thomas at work regarding my news – dear old fuddy-duddy Ron, who's not forgotten my aborted engagement to Laurie.

"You're not rushing into things again are you Molly?"

I bristle, but smile sweetly.

"Oh no, no, *no* Ron. This time it's for real."

At Garland's Maria gushes over me while Theo shakes his head in his usual wicked way and makes suggestive comments. I like Theo but he does have this knack of making me feel terribly young and inexperienced.

Sunday 19 August 1956

Two years ago today we arrived and now we are free agents. How ironic though the way things are turning out. All those hours of discussing travel plans with my friends – the running down to this shipping company and that, either to book a voyage or cancel it – now abandoned and each of us going our separate ways. Ken tells me that Lorna and Athol are delighted at news of our engagement. He didn't mention us going to Australia; that can come later, but I feel sure they won't approve.

Wednesday 29 August 1956

Today Grace drops her bombshell. It seems Geurt has been worried that if she gets back with her family, she won't want to return to New Zealand to marry him. The upshot of this is that she's cancelled her voyage home. This has not been an easy decision for her, but Geurt must come first. They also plan to marry at the end of the year.

Friday 31 August 1956

Why does everything happen at once? With an in-tray piled high with typing and several pages of shorthand to transcribe, I take a call from Maria at Garland's –

"Molly, we're terribly short-staffed at lunchtime and I'm wondering if you and Terry can give us a hand for an hour?"

We both turn up at 12.30 and are run off our feet. This is followed by another three hours of frantic typing back at the office before returning to the restaurant at 5 p.m. Phew, what a day – and tomorrow we're at the Trots again in Lower Hutt.

Saturday 1 September 1956

The momentum continues. Terry and I work non-stop at the racecourse, serving tea and clearing tables. We're exhausted, but the money is lovely and, what's more, they want us here again next Saturday.

This evening Ken and I discuss wedding plans. I found out during the week that the *Monowai* sails from Wellington for Sydney on Friday 30 November so I make a suggestion – how about getting married on Thursday the 29th, spend the night in a hotel and make the four-day trip to Sydney our honeymoon? Ken thinks this is a great idea.

"And what about treating ourselves and going first-class?" I add

"But Molly….."

I know he's going to raise the subject of money, but I squash his objections. On Monday I'll pop down to the shipping company and secure our passages with a deposit. This is one booking that I know for sure will not be cancelled. Sydney, here we come!

Saturday 8 September 1956

Unusually, I oversleep and nearly miss the bus to the races. Terry has just about given up on me. She's cranky and I'm lethargic. Obviously we have not recovered from yesterday when we did hectic lunchtime and evening shifts at Garland's. This is not a good start to another busy day and catastrophe awaits. Before I've had time to clear a table, this snooty-looking woman in smart grey suit sits down with her husband. In my rush to get things shipshape, I knock over a half-filled cup of tea which splashes onto her skirt. If looks could kill…. I'm reduced to a wreck.

"Oh my God, I'll get a cloth – *I'm terribly sorry, please forgive me.*"

But this is not a woman to be placated with profuse apologies or my mounting distress. As I dab away she glares at me ferociously and I'm blinded with tears. Terry shrugs it off.

"It was only a spot or two," she says on the bus back to Wellington, "anyway she was a real cow."

Friday 14 September 1956

Historic day – Jenny departs on the train to Auckland where tomorrow she'll go aboard the *Mataroa* for her trip back to England. How disappointed I am that she's not sailing from Wellington. I had so looked forward to streamers and *Now is the Hour* and everyone waving as the ship cast anchor. At least I've been given an hour off from work to say goodbye at the station. As she steps up into the carriage and the whistle blows I can only wonder *when* and *where* we shall meet again and *what* will have happened to us in the meantime.

Friday 21 September 1956

I experience another waitressing disaster, but this time at Garland's. Scurrying down the aisle, balancing plates and, as always, worryingly conscious of the queue forming down the stairs, I collide with Terry coming in the other direction. At that precise moment one of our most pleasant and courteous young male customers turns to smile up at me, unaware that the jolt has tipped the contents of one of my plates down the back of his raincoat. I'm overcome with horror, anguish, embarrassment and promise over and over again that we'll get it cleaned as soon as possible. Amazingly, he doesn't seem too perturbed. As I rush through to the kitchen I decide that if Maria will not pay for the cleaning, I'll fork out myself. However, she's sympathetic and on my insistence goes out and has a word with him. For the rest of the evening I proceed with caution. Just before closing time Ken comes in for a meal.

"It's bucketing down out there," he says.

Oh dear, my poor customer without any protection, then the oddest thing happens. On our way to the cinema I see him standing at a bus stop in another raincoat, albeit a shabby one. He even nods and smiles at me and I tell Ken about the incident.

Wednesday 26 September 1956

Mum is 54 today. It sounds so *old*. By the time I'm that age, I hope to be a famous writer.

This afternoon Ken rings to say that Lorna and Athol have invited us over for a curry (Lorna's specialty) on Saturday to celebrate our engagement. Inwardly I groan at the prospect, but positively relish the thought of telling them that we're not staying in New Zealand after we're married.

Friday 28 September 1956

How relieved I am to hand over a clean raincoat to my young man in Garland's. He sweeps aside further apologies and says it was just one of those things. Apart from the childish youths who work overtime at the Post Office, Terry and I have some really super male customers, in particular one white-haired guy. He always shows such interest in us both and loves to hear about our latest plans. Somehow this sort of attention and indeed appreciation of the service we give makes the job worthwhile.

Saturday 29 September 1956

To be fair to Lorna and Athol they do make us very welcome again and Lorna puts on a splendid Indian-styled meal, the table beautifully laid out with plates of poppadums and little dishes of this and that to go with the curry. The reaction to the news that we're going to Australia is exactly what I thought it would be. Athol is thunderstruck.

"What on earth do you want to go *there* for?"

"Surely," Lorna says, "it would be better to get yourselves established here first. You can always go there for a holiday later on."

Athol backs her up.

"The Aussies are a tough lot you know – very different from us, not easy to get on with I hear."

"But we're not planning to settle over there," I pipe up. "I've promised Mum and Dad we'll return to England after a couple of years."

This is considered an even greater folly.

"Oh you won't be able to settle back in the old country. You wait and see – you'll be back here in a trice."

It's time to change the subject. What's the point of arguing with people who have absolutely no spark of adventure or romance in their souls? But then, over tea and cake when Ken explains that we'll be having a registry office wedding and drinks for a few friends in a hotel afterwards, Lorna asks why go to all that expense?

"I would be very happy to lay on a little do for you here."

"It can be our wedding present," says Athol.

Moreover, they also promise to be at the Registry Office to act as our witnesses and Athol says he'll bring a tape recorder so we can send a message to Mum and Dad. If, initially, I buck at the idea, I warm to it when I think of the money and the trouble it would save, so I join with Ken in thanking them and the matter is settled.

Friday 5 October 1956

Oh dear, unwanted drama at Garland's. I'm never at ease when the old man is in the kitchen and tonight, with me in pre-menstrual mood, we clash. It starts when I put in an order for steak with tomatoes and onions.

"We haven't got any tomatoes," says Theo.

I point to a large bowl by the side of him.

"We're not using those."

"But Theo, I've already told the customer they're on the menu. I can't possibly…."

The old man approaches.

"Didn't you hear what Theo said?"

"Yes, but I can't go back on my word. Why can't we use those, anyway?"

Maria pulls a face, knowing I suppose that the old man is about to erupt. Suddenly it's all out war.

"I'm sick to death of you, young lady," he yells, "I run this place not you and if you don't like it, you can get out."

Sick to death of me after all these months of faithful service? Seldom do I lose my temper, but now rise to the occasion.

"Okay – I'll leave RIGHT NOW."

"And don't come back," he shouts after me as I run up the stairs to change.

Tears stream down my face as I walk along the street. I've just got to talk to someone. Grace is out with Geurt, so

I decide to take the tram and try and find Ken's place. He's stunned to see me, especially in such a state and we go out for coffee at the nearest milk bar. On and on I babble about the injustice of it all, how awful it is for something like this to happen when we need every penny. He tells me not to worry, but then I start to feel guilty at having left poor Terry and Maria to sort out all my orders. It will take me a long time to recover from this.

Monday 8 October 1956

I meet Terry for lunch and say how sorry I was to leave her in the lurch on Friday. She agrees that old man Garland is impossible and Maria was furious with him. This is some consolation, but I'm bitterly regretting the loss of earnings for the next few weeks.

Wednesday 10 October 1956

My stomach churns when I hear Maria's voice on the phone. Before I can say anything, she's apologising on behalf of her father.

"He had no right to speak to you like that, but you know what his temper is."

I tell her how hurt I was because I've always been so loyal to Garland's and worked very hard. She endorses that and says that she and Theo very much appreciate both Terry and me.

"And that's why I'm ringing. We'd love you to come back. Would you consider it?"

All I need is her assurance that things will be all right with the old man. Yes, she's already spoken to him, so I agree to go in on Monday.

Saturday 20 October 1956

Grace is out all day at Thwaites and, having promised to put some of Ken's shirts in with my washing, I bag the copper early. Stuffing it all in, I then go back to the room and get lost in my book. On returning to the kitchen I find to my dismay that the copper has boiled over and the floor is awash. The task of mopping up is horrendous, but that is only part of my woes. Lifting the lid I shriek with horror which brings forth Jonesie and Rita. Everything is dyed a rosy hue.

"Oh my God – look at this will you?" I say, hoisting out on a stick one item after another, including the culprit, my bright pink gloves.

The girls think it funny but I'm mortified. As much as I'm grieved about Ken's shirts, I'm upset that one of my favourite dresses – the full-skirted white cotton adorned with floral sprigs – is ruined.

"I'll take your shirts to the cleaners to see if they can do anything with them," I promise a bemused Ken when he arrives this afternoon.

Friday 26 October 1956

Although excitement constantly surges through me at the

thought of being on a ship again and seeing Australia, I've taken to waking up in the early morning filled with panic and doubt about getting married. What worries me more than anything is the lack of physical attraction I feel towards Ken. Surely this isn't right? But then, maybe I reason, it's just nerves. I am very edgy at the moment.

As much as I loathe hats (apart from big, face-framing ones), I feel obliged to wear one for the wedding, so tonight after Garland's I purchase the smallest I can find – a top-of-the-head thing with a net to pull over my face and a feather stuck across it horizontally.

Saturday 27 October 1956

Back from a hectic day at the Trots, I come over hot and giddy. Next thing I know I'm flat out on the hall floor, surrounded by concerned faces, including the landlady who Jonesie in a panic decided to inform. Suddenly I have to make a dash for the bathroom where I'm violently sick.

"Shall we get a doctor?" Rita asks when I emerge.

Still pale and shaken I tell them I'll be okay and explain I've been working too hard. I can see though that the landlady doesn't believe me. Instinctively it dawns on me that she thinks I'm pregnant and how ever much I prattle on, she won't be convinced. She makes me feel dirty.

Monday 12 November 1956

At long last there's a letter from Jenny. It leaves me drooling. Frits surprised her by being at Southampton when the

Mataroa docked and a few days later he whisked her off to the Black Forest in Germany. How fabulous! I'm sure she's got a fantastically exciting life ahead of her. Let's hope mine follows suit. As much as I long to see Australia I shall be thrilled to get back to London eventually and explore Europe. Oh how I *pity* all those poor girls who just get married and settle down!

Friday 16 November 1956

Two weeks today it will be streamers and *Now is the Hour* and friends waving us goodbye as we set sail for Australia. The thought takes my breath away. Nevertheless, I shall be sad to say goodbye to Grace, Shirley and Terry with whom I've shared so much these past two years and had such fun. It's a shame, too, that I won't be here for their respective weddings, which will all take place before the end of the year. Still I'm sure we'll keep in touch and meet again sometime.

At Garland's tonight our white-haired gentleman customer takes Terry and me aside and presents each of us with an envelope containing £5 – our wedding present, he says. This is extremely generous of him and we're touched. Lots of other customers, who know of our plans and have always commented on our efficiency and cheerfulness, also wish us well.

Friday 23 November 1956

This is my last day in the office. There's been so much to do this last week that I've been living on my nerves and hardly noticing the time passing. Not much work is done today though and mid-afternoon there's a presentation in the canteen of a beautiful paua shell clock. I feel very emotional making my farewell speech, telling them how much I'll treasure the clock and how much I've enjoyed working with them all.

"The very best two years of my life so far."

There's warm applause, mutterings of how much I shall be missed and everyone shaking my hand. I want to cry. Then, tonight it's farewell to Garland's, another emotional occasion. Theo's eyes twinkle when he hands over their wedding present (a set of towels) and Maria, hugging me tight, is near to tears.

Wednesday 28 November 1956

Last weekend the room in Hawker Street looked a right mess as Grace and I sorted and packed clothes, books, pots and pans and all the other paraphernalia we've accrued. Now, today, with my trunk dispatched to the wharf and Grace departed – she's staying with Geurt's sister until her own wedding – a horrible feeling of desolation comes over me. As I found out long ago there's nothing more demoralising than being home alone on a weekday when everyone is at work. The silence becomes oppressive and I drop down into a pit of depression, life suddenly seeming empty and meaningless. *Meaningless*? Good heavens, girl, pull yourself together – the day after tomorrow you're going to Australia.

Thursday 29 November 1956

The Registry Office ceremony is at 2 p.m. and Ken will pick me up in a taxi at 1.30. The hours stretch endlessly ahead. What can I do with myself till then? Never in my life have I felt so tense and restless. I smoke endless cigarettes as over and over again I ask myself whether I'm doing the right thing marrying this man. Try as I might to reassure myself that these are normal pre-wedding nerves, my panic grows, even when it's time to get dressed.

Of course I'm ready far too early, so I pace up and down the hall watching from the landing window for Ken's arrival. When that moment comes and I see him step out of the car, the thing I notice is that his new suit doesn't sit properly on the shoulders. I feel intensely irritated and – as ridiculous as it may seem – it's enough to bring home to me that without doubt I'm doing the wrong thing. Oh, if only I had the courage to run away now, but I can't, can I?

Just think of Australia, I tell myself, as we set off for the Registry Office.